Lvov Ghetto Diary

DAVID KAHANE

Lvov Ghetto Diary

Translated by Jerzy Michalowicz
Foreword by Erich Goldhagen

The University of Massachusetts Press
Amherst

Copyright © 1990 by David Kahane
Foreword © 1990 by
The University of Massachusetts Press
All rights reserved
Printed in the United States of America
Originally published in Hebrew, in Israel, by Yad Vashem
LC 90–11042
ISBN 0–87023–726–8
Designed by Edith Kearney
Set in Linotron Granjon by Keystone Typesetting, Inc.

Library of Congress Cataloging-in-Publication Data

Kahana, David, 1903–
    [Yoman geṭo Levov. English]
    Lvov ghetto diary / David Kahane ; translated by Jerzy Michalowicz;
    foreword by Erich Goldhagen.
        p.   cm.
    Translation of: Yoman geṭo Levov.
    ISBN 0–87023–726–8 (alk. paper)
    1. Jews—Ukraine—L'vov—Persecutions.   2. Holocaust, Jewish
(1939–1945)—Ukraine—L'vov—Personal narratives.   3. Kahana, David,
1903– .   4. Rabbis—Ukraine—L'vov—Biography.   5. L'vov
(Ukraine)—Ethnic relations.   I. Title.
    DS135.R93L89513   1990
    947'.718—dc20   90–11042
                                                        CIP

British Library Cataloguing in Publication data are available.

❧ CONTENTS

❧ FOREWORD

Because there have been other accounts of the fate of the Jews in the city of Lvov and the Janowski camp, the question naturally arises, Does this memoir add significantly to the stock of our knowledge? I would unhesitatingly answer the question in the affirmative. The *Lvov Ghetto Diary* contains numerous vignettes and details not to be found elsewhere. Its descriptions of the temper and behavior of Nazi executioners are especially valuable; they provide fresh material for the most important and unending scholarly task of understanding the social psychology of the murderers and torturers of European Jewry. But the chief virtue of the memoir lies in its contribution to the historiography of one of the most bitterly disputed aspects of the Holocaust, namely, the attitude of Ukrainians to Jews during that period.

It is an axiom among Jews, and especially among Jewish survivors of the Holocaust, that the vast majority of the Ukrainians, particularly in Galicia, watched the extermination of the Jews with approval and that many actively aided the Nazis in their slaughter. This collective condemnation of the Ukrainian people (vehemently rejected by most Ukrainians) acknowledges that there were exceptions—a minority of Ukrainians were filled with compassion for the Jews and a minuscule number were Good Samaritans aiding and rescuing Jews at the risk of their own lives. The most eminent figure in that minority was Metropolitan Sheptytskyi, the head of the Ukrainian church. Grieving at the slaughter of the Jews and distressed that members of his own people participated in it, he issued a pastoral letter "Thou shalt not murder" (reproduced in this book) and took the audacious step of addressing a letter to Himmler protesting the extermination. No other ecclesiastical figure of equal rank in the whole of Europe displayed such sorrow for the fate of the Jews and acted so boldly on their behalf. Sheptytskyi also saved the lives of Jews by hiding them in monasteries under his control, and one of those thus saved was the author of this memoir. Kahane's account of his hiding, his discussion of Ukrainian–Jewish relations, his conversations with Sheptytskyi, his sketches of the priests, monks, and nuns, of their humanity and their cool and efficient manner in the face of mortal danger to themselves during German searches for hidden Jews, all form an important addition to the theme of the "Righteous Gentiles" in the literature on the Holocaust.

Even historians will read this book with profit. Lay readers are likely to find it irresistibly engaging.

Erich Goldhagen
Lecturer on Jewish Studies
Harvard University
January 1990

PREFACE

I began to write these notes on September 26, 1943, while hiding in the palace of Metropolitan Andrei Sheptytskyi in Lvov, nearly four months after the liquidation of the Lvov ghetto, and after the terrible massacre in the Janowski camp. Most of these pages were written there and in the Studite monastery at Piotr Skarga Street. Events, people, and spectacles of horror reappeared vividly before my eyes. That which I saw and heard, together with what I went through in the monastery itself, I set down on paper, keeping in mind Job's servant's words, "And I only am escaped alone to tell thee" (Job 1:16).

Thirty-five years have passed since I began writing these pages. For various reasons, which I will not elaborate here, I have not published them. By the grace and mercy of God, I came out of hell with my health and spirit intact. Together with my family, I came to Israel, sent down my roots here, was privileged to observe the commandment of settling the Land of Israel, and served my country and my state to the best of my understanding. Today, as then, I confront two grave and difficult questions which call for most rigorous and strict answers.

First, if I ask (and the question would be all the more poignant when asked by those who were not there) what happened and how, I will be able to tell what I saw. The task of rendering tangible the meaning of the Holocaust for those who did not experience it, however, remains insurmountable. The Holocaust defies comprehension. It is beyond my abilities to understand what happened; no one can understand it and make others understand. Our Sages of Blessed Memory established this great rule: "Judge not your fellow man until you stand in his place" (Aboth 2:4). But how does one get to a place where one can understand, clarify, and judge? After all, even we, who were there in this "place," stumble when called upon to understand and to judge. How did it happen that millions died and were exterminated by all manner of bizarre and cruel methods while the whole world stood silent? More than that, when I review the Jewish press in the Land of Israel and in the free world from the period of the Holocaust, I fail to find any proper or deep relation to the events then occurring in the occupied countries. From the perspective of today, the handful of news items and articles published on the subject appear as mere lip service. What I do find are big announcements of balls and festivities taking place as if nothing had happened and there were nothing new under the sun. How was it possible? After all, at that time people knew that was befalling us.

The second question is more like a puzzlement, confusion, and cause of wonder. Although it does not seem reasonable that a believing Jew will repudiate the principle of Divine Providence active in the world, the question nonetheless arises, How do we go about understanding and interpreting the ways of Providence during the Holocaust? How do we accept, understand, and interpret the words of the master of prophets in the song Haazinu (give ear): "He is the rock, his work is perfect; for all his ways are judgment; a God of truth and without iniquity, just and right is he" (Deuteronomy 32:4).

Some endeavor to explain the horrors of the Holocaust as being a punishment inflicted upon European Jewry for the sin of assimilation they had committed. Others try to resolve their bewilderment by conceiving the ways of Providence in terms of the workings of human reason and mind. The prophet had in mind both the former and the latter when he said: "For my thoughts are not your thoughts, neither are your ways my ways, saith the Lord. For as the heavens are higher than the earth, so are my ways higher than your ways, and my thoughts than your thoughts" (Isaiah 55:8–9).

It seems that our generation should give up attempting to provide an answer based on logic and reason. We must reconcile ourselves to the fact that the Holocaust will remain an opaque, horror-ridden riddle conceived by the Creator. The term "Holocaust" intimates but does not express the depths and scale of the disaster.

Tel-Aviv, Zahala

Lvov Ghetto Diary

❧ THE BEGINNING

Lvov

Today is Sunday morning, September 26, 1943. I am at a place called Jura Mountain, in the archbishop's palace of the metropolitan of Lvov, Andrei Sheptytskyi. It has been two weeks since I was transferred here from an attic in the Studite monastery at Piotr Skarga Street. The abbot had learned of a search to be conducted in his monastery. Taking precautions, he decided to transfer me for the time being to a safe house. So now I am sitting in a large library room on the ground floor. The windows face a vast garden which surrounds the palace and the cathedral on three sides. My eyes insatiably drink in the glorious colors spread by the sun in rich profusion. I am hard pressed to forget that for the last four months, that is, throughout the summer, I have seen no green vegetation or the shape of a flower. I arrived here on Monday, May 24, 1943, straight from the camp and on June 2, at night, I was transferred to an attic in the Studite monastery. Since then I have not seen anyone except the man who has been bringing my food.

It is a lovely sunny morning, awash with light, as beautiful as a day can be in our parts, in Podolia, in early fall. It my calculations are correct, today Jews rise at dawn to say Selikhoth [penitential prayers]. I am not certain about my calculations but according to the thousand-year calendar given to me by an old man in the camp last winter, the first day of Rosh Hashanah [Jewish New Year] falls on September 30. Besides, the whole matter seems a bit ridiculous to me since the question is, Are there any Jews left in the world? Are there any people left, free to come and go as they wish? Do Jews still rise to say Selikhoth somewhere? I am longing so much for the heart-warming melody of Selikhoth. It reminds me of Grzymalow (Rymalow), my native town, a remote settlement in the black fertile fields of Podolia. Synagogue beadles who used to wake up people for Selikhoth with a penetrating sorrowful melody materialize before my eyes. From my childhood, before the First World War, I remember Moshe, the synagogue beadle. He used to wake us up with a special wooden clapper, sending muffled, anxious sounds through the empty and silent Jewish alleys:

Rise up, rise up holy people
Rise up, rise up to do the Creator's work
Rise up, rise up, for that purpose thou has been created.

Moshe's successor, Herzli the beadle, or, as I used to call him, "Herzli the hobbler," would intone a different song. He didn't have a clapper and would knock with his stick on the garden fences. He sang better than his predecessor, his voice lamenting and a bit nasal:

Rise up, kosher Jews, dear Jews;
Rise up for Selikhoth.
Rise up, rise up, for that purpose thou has been created.

The third beadle I remember, Avraham Koyl was his name, was a thoroughly prosaic man, a bit of a storekeeper, a bit of a *melamed* [teacher], a bit of a beadle. "So much work," he used to say, "that you can't see the blessings." His predecessors were luckier than he. Both drew their last breath in their beds and found rest in the cemetery of Grzymalow, whereas his bones lie scattered in Belzec.

I have a small daughter by the name of Ruth. She is now four years and three months old. I would gladly tell her all about it; she can understand everything. In her short life she has gone through more than a centenarian. But she is far away from me, in a convent, where she hears other distant sounds, so different from the melodies of Selikhoth. She knows, however, that she is a daughter of Israel and understands her situation full well. How did she get there? And how did I get here, in the archbishop's palace? This is the story I relate in the following pages.

I ✤ THE GHETTO PERIOD

The Occupation and
Annihilation of the
Lvov Community

The First Days

On June 22, 1941, war broke out between Germany and the Soviet Union. It was Sunday, a splendid early summer day. Air raids on the Skanilow airport had begun during the night. My daughter had come down with whooping cough and we had sent her, together with her beloved aunt, to Obroszyn, two train stops from Lvov. The girl recovered in the Obroszyn woods and her heavy cough stopped. I was seized by despair on that Sunday. I didn't know what to do. How would I go about retrieving the child from Obroszyn? I decided to set out on foot. My father-in-law, who loved his first granddaughter deeply, joined me on the hard trek. We had to make a detour around Skanilow, which was being subjected to relentless bombardment by German aircraft. With considerable effort and at great risk, we succeeded in bringing the girl back to Lvov toward evening. For the next week we stayed in the cellar.

Day after day German aircraft raided the city. The Soviet troops beat a slow retreat and on July 1, 1941, the Germans entered Lvov. The Jews were overcome with terror. We were well informed of what had taken place in all the large Polish cities, the terrible pogroms staged by the Germans shortly after their arrival. The horrors perpetrated by them in Lvov, however, were to surpass our wildest imaginings. No one had guessed the enormity of the defeat and the thoroughness of the extermination.

In the interwar period Lvov had been a major Polish city, with sizable Jewish and Ukrainian minorities. From the middle of September 1939 until June 1941, when the Germans invaded the Soviet Union and the great war broke out, Lvov formed part of the Polish territory annexed by the Soviet Union.

At the time of the German occupation some 135,000 Jews lived in Lvov. Among them were scores of refugees who had fled that part of Poland that had become the General Government as early as September 1939, before the advancing Germans. The Jewish population of the city was swelled by many Jews who had come here from district towns during the Soviet rule. Never before had there been so many Jews in Lvov. Such a large Jewish concentration must have been a vexing sight for the Germans.

Everything began on Wednesday morning, July 2. The retreating Soviets left behind three prisons: the so-called Brygidki, a prison overflowing with prisoners, located at Kazimierzowska Street; the prison at the former police headquarters on Lecki Street; and the prison at the former military headquarters on Zamarstynowska Street. Their population consisted mostly of criminals and political prisoners from the Lvov area. Many of them had been executed and buried in the prison courtyard. The Germans opened the prisons wide and released their inmates.

The Gestapo decided to reap a propaganda benefit from the release of prisoners. For that purpose, Lvov Jews were to dig up the graves in the presence of a special commission, the work would be photographed, and the German propaganda machine would thereby acquire first-class material. They would be able to tell the whole world: "Look at the Jewish-Bolshevik murderers whom we have just caught red-handed. Behold their luckless innocent victims!"

After that, all hell broke loose. The Germans seized Jews in their homes and on the streets and forced them to work in the prisons. For that purpose they called upon the services of the Ukrainian police force, which they had set up recently. The Polish and Ukrainian populace rendered whole-hearted assistance to the Germans. The job was completed within three, perhaps four days. Every morning over one thousand Jews were assembled and would then be split up among the three prisons. Several hundred were put to work right away breaking open the concrete floors and removing the corpses. Other Jews were packed into a small courtyard or some prison cell and shot. Not all the unlucky ones who were assigned the job of opening the graves returned to their homes. Some, having fainted from the stench from the graves, were dragged out and shot immediately. There were cases of infections in the Brygidki. Wearing gas masks, the German taskmasters, officers and soldiers, strolled among the Jewish workers with taunting cries such as "sweet is the vengeance." Great crowds of the "Aryan" residents of

Lvov attended this horrendous spectacle. The prison square, the court-yard, the hallways were filled with people who looked on with gleeful satisfaction and with an unconcealed *Schadenfreude*. From time to time hysterical voices could be heard: "Shoot them, the murderers!" Here and there a hand rose to help a German hit the Jews.

In the first days of the occupation, over three thousand Jews perished in the Lvov prisons. Among them was one of the most well-known and respected rabbis of Lvov, Dr. Ezekiel Lewin, and his brother, the rabbi of Rzeszow, Aharon Lewin.

The story of Rabbi E. Lewin's death is puzzling. With the arrival of the Germans, Lvov became a scene of Ukrainian outbursts. According to information arriving from the district towns, the Ukrainians staged horrifying riots against the Jews. Rabbi Lewin resolved to appeal to the Ukrainian metropolitan, Archbishop Andrei Sheptytskyi, who had acquired a reputation as a friend of the Jews and who never concealed his positive attitude toward Judaism. On July 2, Wednesday morning, accompanied by two representatives of the Jewish community, Rabbi Lewin set out for Jura Mountain. The metropolitan received him immediately, promising to write a pastoral letter in which he would warn the Ukrainians against committing murder and looting. He admitted, however, that there was nothing he could do concerning the actions of the Germans.

As they were parting, the archbishop suggested that Rabbi Lewin stay in his residence awhile longer, as he had heard that the streets were unsafe. At that time another Jew, Rabbi Lilienfeld of Podhajce, an old friend of the Sheptytskyi family, was present in the metropolitan's residence. Rabbi Lewin thanked him for the offer but turned it down. A priest waited for him at the gate to escort him to his apartment at 3 Kollataj Street. As they passed the "Warszawa" cafe, Rabbi Lewin refused further escort and parted from the priest. At the gate of his house he met a Jewish woman whom he knew who lived in the same house (the women had not yet been hurt). She told him that Ukrainian policemen were in the house, seizing Jews for work in the Brygidki prison. She suggested that he come to her apartment where she would conceal him, along with her husband, in a safe hideout they had built there. With incomprehensible obstinacy Rabbi Lewin turned down this offer too and started climbing the stairs to his apartment. As he reached the door, two Ukrainian policemen came out and took him with them. He did not return. His eldest son, Kurt Lewin, who had been taken earlier to the Brygidki, returned home in the evening. He said that he had seen his father at ten or eleven in the morning being led into the courtyard. That was the last time he was seen alive.*

The location of Rabbi Lewin's grave came to light only in January 1942. Two members of the synagogue board, Dr. Reiss (nicknamed "small" Reiss) and Shargel, brought two witnesses to the rabbinate. They were refugees from Krakow, reliable people who related the following:

A number of people were taken off their work crew to bury all the Jews murdered during the day in the Brygidki. They were not beaten, just told to pile the Jewish bodies into a heap. Toward evening, when everybody had dispersed, these Jews were locked in a cell. At night, in pitch dark, they were told to leave the cell and ordered to remove the corpses laying outside. A truck was standing at the gate. When the corpses were loaded onto it, the two were seated next to the driver to help him with the burial.

Before the truck started on its way the driver told them: "Do you know whom we are carrying in the truck? Why, your rabbi." With a flashlight he illuminated the face of one of the corpses. They recognized Rabbi Lewin instantly; the man was a well-known figure in Lvov. The black priestly robes he had been wearing when leaving the archbishop's residence were stained with blood. The driver took the truck to Holoko [Holosko]. In a field adjoining the woods, a large pit had been dug where all the bodies were buried. The witnesses described to us in detail the location of the grave. This testimony was collected by Rabbi Israel Leib Wolfsberg, Rabbi Dr. Kalman Chameides, and me. The testimony was deposited at the archives of the Jewish Court located at Bernstein Street, the former location of *Yad Harutzim*.

From Tuesday until Sunday I hid in the cellar of my apartment at Tokarzewski Street. The cellar was ingeniously concealed by a wooden partition and the henchmen who had called on the place several times had failed to spot it. Apart from me, Dr. Herman Pfeper, a journalist on the staff of the *Nowy Dziennik* (Daily news), and an assistant of Dr. Yehoshusah Thon of Krakow stayed in the cellar.

Today, surveying the events in Lvov from the perspective of time, my heart still trembles with terror. Cynically, murderously, cold bloodedly, the Germans put into effect their plan to exterminate the Jews. They planned their moves like a military operation. With calculated German precision they planned each step from the strategic point of

---

*See Appendix 1: Two Accounts of Rabbi Lewin's Death.

view, from the first atrocities in the prisons until the final liquidation of the Lvov ghetto. Everything was planned ahead of time with the aim of breaking the Jews physically, morally, and spiritually, and of leading them step by step into disaster.

The period of relative calm that set in after the events in the prisons lasted several days. Driven out of their homes by hunger, the Jews began appearing on the streets. As soon as they appeared, the Germans started abducting men and women and transferring them to Pelczynska Street. A large building stood there which the Lvov municipality had erected shortly before the war to house the municipal power station. At this time the building was used as Gestapo headquarters. The prison at Lecki Street was just a few steps away. The names Pelczynska Street and Lecki Street instilled terror in all Jews. Everyone trembled with fear at these words.

Only a handful of the scores of unfortunates who were brought there ever returned home. They were stunned and struck dumb as if by a magic spell. Human imagination could not conceive the tortures these poor wretches were subjected to.

On July 15, announcements were posted on walls throughout the city with the "armband" (*opaska* in Polish) decree. Every Jew, including Catholics whose Jewish ancestry could be traced back to the third generation, was required to wear a "Jewish armband" on the right sleeve—a Star of David painted blue on a piece of white fabric. From that moment on each Jew was branded with an identifying mark. The armband singled out its owner like an animal and whoever wanted to was allowed to beat or murder him with impunity. In district towns the curse of the armband was easier to bear. The Jewish populace there got used to it quickly. A Jew caught without it paid a fine and that was it. In Lvov the whole business was much more serious. The main streets were always filled with military personnel and SchuPo (*Schutz-Polizei*) policemen swarmed everywhere. Who could let the chance go by of slapping a Jew wearing his provocative armband? Once I watched from my window a SchuPo man posted at the corner of Tokarzewski and Bem streets. Bored by the assignment, he started dealing blows with his rubber truncheon to every Jew who passed his way from either street. His method was as follows: when a Jewish passerby failed to greet him, he would say: "Why didn't you greet me, you dog?" If the Jew did greet him, he would say: "Why did you greet me, you dog?" and tear the Jew's hat off and give him a bloody beating with his truncheon in the bargain. I stood at the window and looked on. This horrifying game lasted for about two hours. In the meantime a crowd of spectators had gathered around the SchuPo man. In vain I looked in their faces for a trace of sympathy. Each expressed satisfaction, every onlooker smirked. At 6:00 p.m. another SchuPo came to relieve him. Proudly he showed his successor a pile of hats in front of him, the "spoil" of one afternoon.

Returning home with a bleeding head was a minor problem, however, compared with what happened to those caught without an armband. Such a man would not return home at all. In no other place was the absence of an armband such a disaster as it was in Lvov. People trembled with fear, trying not to forget to wear it. This fear was exemplified by the fact that in each apartment a big notice was posted on the back of the front door saying, in German and Polish: "Remember the armband!" People would sew an armband on each set of clothing, lest they forget to transfer it when changing clothes. In their naïveté they believed that the Germans were looking only for Jews without armbands. At that point we still didn't know that the armband was just the beginning.

Throughout the summer "round-ups for forced labor" were carried on. Every morning the Germans took away hundreds of Jews to perform various tasks. The work was unproductive, unplanned, and disorganized. Its purpose was to oppress the Jew, torment him, enslave him, and constrict him.

On one occasion I was seized at my house for work at Kordecki Street. A large wooden shack for storing various military supplies had once stood there. During the air raids on Lvov it had burnt to the ground. The place was full of charred wood, burned iron, and nails. Several young Ukrainian policemen put six Jews to work there. They looked at their watches and announced: "The place must be cleaned up in two hours. Woe to anyone who uses a spade or even a piece of tin." It was a hot summer day, the sun beat on our heads mercilessly. It seemed to me that we stood no chance of cleaning up the place with just our bare hands. But, as it turned out, a human being is stronger than iron. Within two hours the place was clean. The Ukrainians, for their part, stood by their word; whoever tried to use a piece of tin or iron felt their boots on his body right away. One Ukrainian said: "One must not waste one's hand to beat a Jew; the Jew must be kicked."

Then the so-called Petlyura days came. The anniversary of the death of Simon Petlyura, *hetman* [chief] of a popular Ukrainian army, falls on July 28. The man had been killed by a Ukrainian Jew by the name of

Schwarzbardt, who shot him in revenge for anti-Jewish outbursts in the Ukraine.

Before I relate the events of the Petlyura days, I must make a few comments on relations between the Jews and the Ukrainians in general. The depth and persistence of Jew-hatred among the Ukrainian people is truly astonishing. Throughout the history of their national movement, every revolt, be it against Russia or against Poland, has always involved the spilling of Jewish blood and anti-Jewish pogroms.

Nearly three hundred years have passed since the Khmelnytskyi uprising, the sanguinary period known in our history as the horrors of '48 and '49, but the nature of the relationship between the two peoples has not changed. In 1918, just as in the days of Khmelnytskyi, the troops of Petlyura launched an assault on Jewish townships in the Ukraine, unleashing a terrible bloodbath. This is also what happened in the summer of 1941. As soon as the Soviet army had retreated from eastern Galicia, the peasants set on the tiny Jewish hamlets and began murdering Jews with unspeakable cruelty. Usually in each band of peasants there were two or three Germans who exploited the peasants' blind hatred of the Jews to incite them even more. I can still see the letter that my eighty-six-year-old mother sent me from my native town of Grzymalow in late June 1941. She wrote that my three brothers, her sons, and an eighteen-year-old grandson perished for Kiddush Hashem [Sanctification of the Name]. She wrote, inter alia: "I do not understand it. Has God let me live so long only so that my old eyes will see my children rolling in their own blood? After all, these were the same peasants who used to visit us, often stayed for a night, traded with my children in a most friendly way, and now these very same peasants took my sons away and butchered them. Almost all the men in the township were shot that day." Where should one look for the root cause of this pervasive, terrible hatred?

This is not the place for a thorough analysis of this question. In my memoirs I will stick to just the bare facts. I relate what my eyes have seen. A few comments are in order, nonetheless.

I cannot say that the Jews are completely blameless. Certainly, a peasant would have been angry with a Jewish land tenant who took a key to the church as a mortgage. More than once a Jewish innkeeper would get a peasant drunk and then swindle him and even steal his property. Nor were the weights and measures used by Jewish store-keepers in small towns always accurate. But how can one blame a whole people for the sins of individual land tenants or storekeepers? "Swindling" by a Jewish storekeeper, who in most cases was as impoverished as anyone, cannot serve as an excuse for a pogrom. After all, there were other merchants in the Ukraine, not Jews, but Christian Armenians. They, like Jews, were foreigners, and the morality of their commercial practices differed little from that of the Jews. Why, then, had "the wrath of the people" never turned against them? In any event, the Ukrainians have won in at least one respect. They have improved their condition considerably. The Jewish innkeeper has disappeared and all Jewish settlements have been eradicated from the face of the earth, the bones of their inhabitants scattered about in Belzec and other camps. Their place has been was taken by a Ukrainian innkeeper and storekeeper. Are their commercial practices on a higher moral level than those of their Jewish predecessors? It doesn't seem so. From what I know, the opposite is true. Against whom will "the wrath of the people" turn now?

I will have committed the sin of partiality and of letting personal grievances get in the way of truth as I see it, however, if I did not point out that large sections of the Ukrainian intelligentsia refrained from taking part in these actions and even fought against the brutal manifestations of the anti-Semitism of their compatriots. I pay homage to the leadership of the Ukrainian priesthood, to scores of monks who took enormous risks in saving Jewish children. I must note with regret, however, that they were the exception rather than the rule.

Ukrainian youths did not seem to be swayed by the pastoral letters of the metropolitan Andrei Sheptytskyi or by the example of monks risking their lives by hiding Jewish children in their monasteries and by bringing food to the wretched Jewish fugitives who had escaped from the camps. They remained under the spell of the nascent Ukrainian nationalist literature, virulent in its vicious anti-Semitism.

Returning to the Petlyura days: even today I do not know who organized these days or, to be exact, who conceived the idea. Did the Gestapo suggest the "brilliant" idea to the Ukrainian militia, or did the Ukrainians conceive of it by themselves as an act of revenge for the death of Petlyura? In any event, on the morning of July 29, Ukrainian policemen swooped down on Jewish houses, removed young Jewish men and women, and marched them to Lecki Street. The operation was repeated throughout that day and the next until the prison was packed with people. Even the prison courtyard swarmed with Jews; only a handful succeeded in getting away. Hair-raising scenes unfolded. No food was brought in. From time to time gangs of Ukrainian policemen burst into the place, dealt blows with rifle butts, and screamed: "This is for our *hetman* Simon Petlyura."

Each visit resulted in broken heads, ribs, and bones. This, however, turned out to be a minor trouble. Petlyura's blood could only be avenged with blood. And this is, in fact, what happened. Several thousand Jews, mostly intelligentsia, did not return home after the Petlyura days. The sites of their shooting and burial remain a secret which they took with them.

The Judenrat and Its Departments

The Gestapo got impatient with handling the Jews on the streets. The front lines kept moving eastward. Slowly the situation became stable. Eastern Galicia was annexed to the General Government as the district of Galicia. The military authorities turned the control of the government over to a civilian administration. The time had come to set up a Judenrat, an organization to deal with the Jewish community. At first the authorities approached Professor Allerhand who had served as head of the Lvov Jewish community for a long time. They demanded that he submit to the German authorities a memorandum on the situation of the Jewish population of Lvov, its material and cultural condition and proposals for the restoration of the Jewish community in the city. They addressed the same questions to other public figures. As Professor Allerhand told me later, all answers amounted to a proposal to set up a legally incorporated religious community as in the past. The Germans, however, looked at it differently. National Socialism regarded the establishment of Judenrats as one of the ways of destroying the Jews and Judaism. The communal structure set up by them led to demoralization, first of its workers and then of the whole community. Simply put, it amounted to but one stage leading toward the annihilation of the entire Jewish population. It formed but one section of the overall "plan" prepared in advance of the "battle" with the Jews.

Such Judenrats had already been set up throughout the General Government. Jews had been completely set apart from the general population, their isolation aimed at preventing them from exerting, God forbid, a bad influence on their neighbors. After a medieval fashion, a Jewish ghetto was set up in every locality, surrounded by a high fence and kept under heavy guard within and without. Only birds enjoyed any freedom of movement between the Aryan district and the ghetto. To do the same a Jew needed a special permit. Staying outside the ghetto without such a permit meant death.

Needless to say, a community sealed off from all sides, as the ghetto was, had to have its own administration. Consequently, a need arose to establish a municipality of sorts. (The Lvov Jews called it the "municipality of bizarre death.")

In the first days of August 1941, the German authorities put announcements on house walls all over town. They proclaimed the establishment of a Judenrat whose official name was *Judische Gemeinde der Stadt Lemberg* (Jewish community of the city of Lemberg [Lvov]). As its first chairman the Germans appointed a well-known Jewish figure from the moderate assimilationists, Dr. Yosef Parnas. The decree also spelled out the principal purposes of the Judenrat:

First, to carry out all orders and regulations of the German authorities pertaining to the Jewish population.

Second, to manage internal relations within the Jewish community; to set up social welfare institutions, hospitals, police (*Ordnungs-Dienst*), etc.

It goes without saying that the first was the most important reason for the Judenrat. The Germans made no attempt to conceal this. On many occasions they said that the Judenrat was but an executive branch of the Gestapo. The second paragraph was of no interest to them at all. They left it to the Jews, and thereby created conditions for abuse and fraud.

Step by step, an extensive communal apparatus was set up with large numbers of people on its staff. At the time of the great *Aktion* in August 1942, when the Jewish community of Lvov numbered over ninety thousand people, the Judenrat staff had reached three thousand.

1. Personnel Department This department was charged with managing the office personnel and with supervising the administrative apparatus. In actual fact it ran the community. From its inception until the liquidation of the ghetto, it was headed by Leon Hoch, a former trustee of the Lodz bank, an effective man with organizational skills.

2. Supplies Department This was the most important of all the departments. The community existed because of "supplies." This department was assigned the responsibility of fulfilling orders placed by various German institutions. Thus the name "Supplies Department" derived from the need to supply the Germans with goods and services. The German institutions and organizations that had moved to Lvov demanded that the Jewish community supply them with everything they wanted. Boldly they demanded items such as furniture, household utensils, clothing, valuables, bedding, kitchen utensils—everything needed by the German officials and their families who had just settled in Lvov. The Supplies Department was obliged to comply with every whim of the most important as well as the lesser officials. The demands included installing a tub or an entire kitchen. Single orders were placed as well: one wanted fancy boots; another, a nice fur; still another, a Persian rug, a piano, English fabric for a suit, a silver fox fur, bric-a-brac, expensive earrings, diamond rings, gold watches, etc. The Supplies Department had to fill requests of all kinds in the hope of containing German wrath. On more than one occasion the military hospital demanded beds, mattresses, sheets, and complete kitchen fixtures.

In the district towns the Judenrat had to attend to the needs of the nascent colony of German officials. Beside the aforementioned articles, for example, it had to outfit a complete kindergarten and furnish the German kindergarten teacher, who had just arrived penniless and barefoot from her ruined homeland, with a dowry of clothing she had never dreamed of. All this amounted to organized plunder; like leeches the Germans attached themselves to the body of the Jewish community and sucked it ravenously, and it seemed they would never be sated.

How did the department manage to procure all these goods? By German decree the Jews were forbidden to own new luxurious furniture. In fact, they were not allowed to keep any piece of furniture without a permit from the city commandant. At that time a mass exodus of Jews from all over the city began, into the Jewish district. Eviction orders already had been served to scores of people and preparations were afoot for the establishment of the ghetto. Upon moving to a new apartment, a Jew was allowed to take with him a table, a simple closet, and a double bed. Even for these meager belongings he needed a special license from the city commandant. Otherwise the authorities could confiscate everything.

Such licenses were issued through the Judenrat. The applicant would submit his request via the Supplies Department by listing on a special form all his furniture and the number in the famly, and then ask permission to transfer such and such pieces of furniture in accordance with official regulations.

Meanwhile officials of the Supplies Department confiscated the remaining furniture and most of the kitchen utensils. Eight to ten days later the permit would be ready and the applicant was allowed to move into his new quarters, which, in any event, did not have enough space for all his furniture.

In order to discharge its obligations, the Supplies Department was obliged to employ a vast staff and dispatch large numbers of agents in order to confiscate mercilessly all the needed goods: furniture and underwear, sheets and bedding, kitchen utensils and crystal vessels. Needless to say, all this activity involved corrupt practices, even outright stealing. Those who knew the agents personally were not hurt. Others paid bribes. Some agents confiscated the goods only to appropriate them for themselves.

The name by which this institution was known in the Jewish street speaks volumes; instead of *Besorgungsamt* (Supplies Department), it was called *Beraubungsamt* (the Plunder Department).

Thus the Jewish community was poisoned; the Germans incited brother against brother, saying "Let the Jews bite each other like dogs."

3. Jewish Police   The third department of the Lvov Jewish community was called Order Service (*Ordnungs-Dienst*)—the Jewish police.

I write about this institution with great anguish and deep shame. Whereas the Supplies Department was forced to hand over Jewish property to the Germans, the *Ordnungs-Dienst,* in the ghetto as the Jewish militia, had to sacrifice Jewish victims to the German Moloch.

At first it seemed that Jewish policemen were indeed charged with keeping public order. Since sooner or later the Jews were scheduled to move to a separate district, i.e., the ghetto, where no German or Ukrainian policemen would enter, there was a need for a local police force. This, in fact, was the job of the Jewish police in all the larger cities of the General Government where uniformed Jewish policemen armed with rubber truncheons kept order within ghetto bounds.

In Lvov, too, Jewish police began playing soldier. Although they did not wear nice uniforms as in other cities, they were furnished with caps modeled after the caps of policemen in prewar Poland. Instead of the Polish eagle, they were adorned with the Star of David bearing the inscription J.O.D. (*Judische Ordnungs-Dienst, Lemberg*). On their right sleeve they wore a yellow armband in the shape of a sleeve cover, with the Star of David on it, the letters J.O.D. and a stamp of the German police. Policemen were exempt from wearing the regular Jewish armband.

At first Jewish police headquarters was located in the Judenrat building at 2 Starotandetna Street. Later, with the establishment of the ghetto, it was split into three commissariats: at Bernstein Street in the former building of *Yad Harutzim*. This building also housed the police headquarters and the Criminal Police (*KriPo*). The second commissariat was located at 112 Zamarstynowska Street, and the third at Zniesienie.

The nature of the task assigned by the Germans to the Jewish police came to light only in late summer of 1941, with the establishment of the first forced-labor camps in the district of Galicia. The Judenrat was required to supply the first quota of Jews for work in the camps. Naturally, the Jewish police were charged with supplying the labor force through seizures.

Although the Jewish police was the instrument of the Judenrat, it received its orders and instructions directly from the Gestapo. Thus it was compelled to carry out all German orders. Dereliction of duty entailed deadly risk to those involved. In order to save their own lives, the policemen had to turn strangers over to the authorities, to deliver their brethren to the butcher's knife. As such actions ran against morality and Jewish law, people of conscience did not join the police. In cases where they had served on the force from the beginning, they did their best to avoid disasters. I knew many policemen who risked their lives to save Jewish families from death. But there were others who demanded payment for rescue. There were also many who turned blackmail into a profession and made a good living out of this ignominious practice.

To me, Jewish policemen in the Lvov ghetto did not appear at all like their prototypes—the policemen in ancient Egypt. The latter did not hand over to the Egyptian Gestapo those of their brethren who failed to produce the required quota of bricks. The Midrash interprets the verse "And the officers of the children of Israel, which Pharaoh's taskmasters had set over them, were beaten" (Exodus 5:14) as meaning that Jewish policemen were risking their lives, beaten and killed by the Egyptian taskmasters, but did not turn over their brethren to their oppressors.

The Jewish police left a permanent stain on the history of the Lvov ghetto.

4. The Housing Department German taskmasters commenced their rule in Lvov by setting up two diametrically contrasting residential districts. One was given over to the ruling caste, the noble German race. The other was meant for Jewish slaves living under the sentence of death. The territory stretching between them, comprising the city center and its suburbs, was designated for the local population—the Poles and Ukrainians.

The German district was located in the best neighborhood of Lvov, near Stryjski Park, on both sides of Potocki, Listopad, Nasza, and Strzech streets (and others). Big blackboards were posted on its borders with a notice: "For Ukrainians and Poles, entrance strictly forbidden!" The Ukrainian and Polish owners of apartments in this area were served with eviction orders. As compensation they were offered Jewish apartments in the mixed Polish-Ukrainian district. The procedure was more or less as follows: an Aryan resident of the would-be-German district would pick out a Jewish apartment and then go to the municipal housing office where he gave the exact address of the apartment of his choice. Thereupon he was given the deed of ownership, or, as it was called, order. The Jewish owner of the spoken for apartment was sent an eviction notice requiring him to move out within three days.

Not only the Aryans evacuated from the German district, however, were entitled to Jewish apartments. Any Aryan who didn't like his own apartment for any reason could also apply. Respectable citizens as well as drunkards, criminals who had lived in cellars all their lives, and peasant vagrants ejected from their own villages had been waiting for just this opportunity. Now their hour had come and they lost no time in seizing it.

The municipal housing office was packed with people. Long lines stretched at the counters, waiting for the "order" desired by everyone. Like a horde of jackals they descended on Jewish apartments and Jewish furniture. Everyone, the self-respecting citizen living on the first or second floor and the basement dweller, was eager to lay his hands on Jewish property. All of them came to the Jews, angrily shoving the order into their hands and screaming: "Move out of the apartment right away! You've been at the top long enough! Now it's time for us!" Where could the luckless evicted Jews go? To the Housing Department of the Jewish community at 2 Starotandetna Street. The Housing Department, however, had begun functioning only recently. The ghetto district had not yet been designated and already hundreds of families without a roof over their heads demanded attention.

For the time being they were directed to the Jewish district, called the "third district," stretching on both sides of Sloneczna, Zokiewska, Zamarstynowska, and Zrodlana streets. However, no vacant apartments could be found there. Those with relatives in the Jewish district somehow managed. Others, mostly Jews from districts taken over by Aryans, had to purchase apartments.

This situation marked the opening of a sad chapter in the history of the Housing Department. Having just been set up and manned, it dispatched its agents to the Jewish district. They would take measurements of an apartment, open a file for each one, and thereby acquire entitlement to each vacant apartment. According to law, each Jew was entitled to three square meters of living space. Later, when the ghetto area became even more constricted, even this meager floor space was reduced to two square meters. Thus twenty-four or twenty-five people were squeezed into a two-bedroom apartment.

It must be admitted that residents of the third district and the Jewish staff of the Housing Department did not display high moral standards. They were inadequate for the task that those critical times had imposed on them.

The residents of the third district, poor and affluent alike, refused to accept subtenants for free. They haggled for each square meter, each bed, each chair. Officials of the Housing Department who had been authorized to straighten out this mess only made it worse. Venality spread far and wide within their ranks. For money one could obtain a seizure order, even against the will of the apartment owner. In such cases the police had to intervene in order to force the owner to transfer his apartment into the hands of the person presenting the seizure order. The spectacle was one of uproar, screams, and even blows.

How was any kind of normal life possible under such circumstances? Could peace and quiet prevail in these cramped, dark, and filthy apartments? These circumstances were casting their heavy black shadow over the life of the ghetto residents. Seeing no way out, no possibility to survive, people succumbed to despair.

5. *Economy Department*   The main task of this department was to secure the supply of food for the Jewish population.

For a short while after the arrival of the Germans, Jews were allowed to make purchases at the general municipal grocery stores. However, they could buy only bread—at first 120 grams, and afterward only 70 grams a day. Others were entitled to 200 grams of bread, as well as other products: a bit of flour, sugar, groats, and occasionally something else. Waiting in line for 70 grams of bread often entailed mortal risks. The Jews were required to stand in a separate line. They would wait on the side, like lepers, until all the Aryans had been served and then, if any bread were left at all, they could make their purchase. Often they would be driven out of the store, spat on, or beaten. More than once, instead of 70 grams of bread, a Jew brought home a broken rib or an open wound.

The news that the Economy Department would be opening special grocery stores for the Jewish populace was received with a measure of relief (the Soviets called these stores *bakalia*). Very soon, however, this news turned out to be a disappointment. The meager supplies that the Germans allocated for the Jewish population disappeared somewhere along the line between the pirates of the Economy Department and the *bakalia,* so that a minuscule portion reached the Jewish customer. Apart from 70 grams of bread, Jews received almost nothing. Once in a very long while they would receive several dozen grams of sugar, a bit of flour gone sour which grated on one's teeth, and, on occasion, several dozen grams of honey substitute. The Economy Department resembled a stock exchange, always with the deafening din of haggling "at the expense of the public." Deals were struck under the patronage of the Judenrat, whereas the Jewish poor, who had no money in their pockets to purchase bread, had bellies swelling with hunger. People often died of starvation. This then was the way the Economy Department operated and, sad as it is, this account accords with the truth.

6. *Labor Department* The sixth department of the Judenrat was entrusted with supplying a Jewish labor force for the Germans. Every day various German institutions requested a certain quota of workers from the Judenrat. In order to avoid seizures of Jews in apartments and on the streets, the Judenrat decided that every Jew would be required to report for work duty once a week. Those unable to work could send a replacement or ransom themselves at the Labor Department, which supplied workers for a fee.

In the course of time, various German institutions, military and civilian, construction companies, and others began demanding that the Labor Department supply them with skilled workers for permanent jobs. Jews were discovered to be a source of excellent and cheap labor. In most cases the Germans paid nothing to these workers, who received their wages from the Judenrat. The Germans paid their permanent Jewish workers half the wages they paid to Aryan workers.

Seeking to control the demand for labor on the part of German institutions, the authorities took over this matter by establishing a Jewish Labor Office as an independent operation headed by the Germans and modeled after the Municipal Labor Office. I shall discuss the activities of this institution later on. Instead of the former Labor Department, the Judenrat was saddled with a department whose job was to collect the wages from the Jewish population and pay those workers in the German institutions who received no salary at all.

Later, when the ghetto was fenced off and the Lvov Jewish community numberd one-third of its original size, the Labor Department became a Cleaning Department charged with cleaning the filthy alleys of the ghetto, removing garbage, and other such jobs.

7. *Tax Department*   This department handled the finances of the Judenrat. The expenditures, as aforementioned, were enormous. The chief leech, the Supplies Department, was insatiable. In addition, outlays had to be budgeted for staff salaries which, although not much per person, amounted to considerable sums of money. Financing all these expenditures necessitated taxation of the Jewish community.

A number of "assessing commissions" were set up to determine the amount of tax to be paid. Their task was to develop an equitable division of the tax burden. Needless to say, the more affluent among the residents sometimes had to be coerced into paying the high tax assessed by these commissions. It must be noted that the Tax Department discharged its responsibilities in an equitable and honorable way.

8. *Sanitation Department*   This department operated under the harshest and most adverse conditions. From scratch, with no outside help whatsoever, it set up three hospitals: at Allembekow Street in the former building of the Trzecki High School; at Kuszewicz Street in the former building of the Fifth Gymnasium; and at 112 Zamarstynowska Street, where a hospital for contagious diseases was located. Apart from these, three clinics operated, dispensing free treatment, as well as a number of health clinics in a number of locations in the ghetto. This entire health complex was established with a few pennies collected from the ghetto residents and a few individual contributions. The authorities took away from us a fully equipped hospital at Rappaport Street and turned it over to the Ukrainians.

One year later, with the reduction of the ghetto area, the authorities wrested two hospitals from us. The Jewish community was left with only one hospital at Kuszewicz Street. The municipal Health Office evinced keen interest in the hospitalization arrangements and medical equipment of the Jewish hospitals, similar to the way the Germans had confiscated Jewish clothing and money.

9. Social Welfare Department   This department operated under conditions identical to those of the Health Department. It received no outside assistance and subsisted on sporadic locations of several thousand zloty from the Judenrat board and on whatever funds it managed to raise among the Jewish populace.

Within ghetto bounds, the Social Welfare Department cooperated with an independent Jewish association for mutual assistance, *Yidishe Sotsiale Aleynhief* (YSA), with headquarters in Krakow. These two bodies did their utmost to ease the hardships of their clients, some of whom received permanent assistance, while others were given only occasional support. Public kitchens and teahouses were set up. These two institutions, however, were incapable of answering the needs of the hungry and suffering population. There was a bottomless well of needs.

10. Justice Department   This department dealt with legal matters within the Jewish community. A special court of law was set up for the Jews, with Jewish notaries and other legal institutions operating in the ghetto. The Justice Department also processed requests and other applications addressed to the German authorities and handled general legal and civil cases, as well as other matters that could not be taken care of within the ghetto. The Justice Department handled these issues through liaison officers who worked with appropriate German institutions.

11. Statistics Department   This department kept accurate records of the Jewish population. The number of bread coupons provided an exact indication of how many Jews resided in the ghetto, as well as the number of those who disappeared after an *Aktion*. From its inception until the liquidation of the ghetto, this department was headed by Dr. Frederyk Katz, a former director of the Statistics Department of the Lvov municipality, a very congenial and civilized man.

12. Construction Department   This department handled the demolition and removal of Jewish-owned buildings and synagogues that had burned. As it performed no constructive work, it was a construction department in name only.

13. Education Department   At first the Jews believed that the Germans would allow at least one elementary school to operate, or would permit some form of group tutoring. No one could have imagined the satanic plan to carry out a total extermination of the Jews, a general liquidation. Despite a strict ban on teaching and education, a small number of pupils received clandestine religious and secular instruction under conditions of great peril for the staff.

14. Burial Department   This particular agency of the Judenrat was never short of work. No other department was as busy as this one. People died in great numbers from hunger, cold, typhoid, epidemics, poverty, and loneliness. After the establishment of the Janowski camp, cartloads of bodies of those shot or tortured to death were brought in daily. The morgue at the old graveyard at Rappaport Street was always full. The courtyard was permanently strewn with corpses covered with canvas sheets, waiting their turn. Carts shuttled from morning till night between the Rappaport Street cemetery and the Pilichowska Street cemetery. These were large simple carts or flatbed wagons, laden with corpses covered with canvas sheets, most of them without coffins, which for most mourners remained an inaccessible luxury. It was impossible to bury each body in a separate grave. The rabbinate allowed mass burials, "one body on top of another."

With the gradual reduction of the ghetto area, the Burial Department moved from one location to another, from Rappaport Street to Kleparow Square and from there to Rekodzielnicza Street. It was the only department that continued to function after the community was dispersed, until the liquidation of the ghetto.

15. Religious Affairs Department   This department was entrusted with the supervision of religious matters within the Jewish population.

The Soviet government had abolished the legally incorporated Jewish religious community (*kehilla*) and the rabbinate ceased to exist as an official body. Rabbi Dr. Levi Freund passed away in April 1941. Rabbi Lewin was murdered, as I have already mentioned, on July 2, 1941, in the Brygidki prison.

With the reorganization of the religious community under way, the chairman, Dr. Parnas, sought to revive its religious institutions. Like other Jews, he believed that the current wave of persecutions would end sometime and that Jewish life and stability would gradually be restored. Acting on this assumption, he set about reorganizing the rabbinate. All the Orthodox rabbis active in the interwar period were still alive. They included Rabbi Moshe Elhanan Alter, a former president of the rabbinical court holding jurisdiction within the city limits; Rabbi Israel Leib Wolfsberg, president of the rabbinical court holding jurisdiction outside the city limits; and the rabbi of Zalozycz, Rabbi Nathan Nute Leiter. The following served as religious judges: Rabbi Shmulke [Samuel] Rappaport and his brother; the judge of Grodecka district (Greidinger), Rabbi Moshe Aharonpreiss; the judge of Zniesienie district, Rabbi Hersh [Rosenfeld]; and the judge of the Zolkiewskie district, Rabbi Anshel Schreiber. The rabbi of the city of Katowice, Dr. Kalman Chameides, and the present author were coopted to the rabbinate. Rabbi Chameides arrived at Lvov as a refugee from Katowice, and I had served as the official rabbi of the Sykstuski synagogue from 1929 to 1939.

However, religious life was not fully renewed. The situation in Lvov in this regard was much graver than in the district towns. Public worship was banned, forcing Jews to gather in private apartments for secret prayer meetings—minyanim. With the discovery of a minyan—usually the Aryan janitor would inform the police—all the worshippers, together with owners of the apartment, would be taken to the Lecki prison. No one ever returned from there. In the initial period after the occupation, the Germans conducted intense searches for rabbis.

Many days passed before the rabbinate decided to appear publicly in the guise of the Religious Affairs Department. This took place in late fall 1941, when the 100,000-strong Jewish community raised demands for kosher meat, sanctification of marriage, and adjudication of divorce cases.

With a heavy heart a rabbi would sign a marriage contract and enter it into the wedding records at the Office of Population Registration. Signing divorce papers to be submitted before a German court posed an even greater danger. By signing a document of this sort a rabbi practically delivered himself into German hands by testifying to the existence of rabbis in Lvov. But he had no choice.

The problem of divorces was particularly painful and tragic. The would-be divorcees were Aryan women who had converted to Judaism, married Jews, and left their past behind. They had borne children and lived happily with their husbands. Suddenly the insane race statutes became the law of the land and demanded that they divorce their husbands—otherwise they would be required to enter the ghetto and wear the identifying armband. In all the divorce proceedings, however, I saw only a handful of women who agreed to part from their Jewish spouses. Usually the husband would plead tearfully with his wife to consent to a divorce to save herself and the children (as half-Aryan, such children were entitled to live in Aryan city districts and were exempt from wearing the Star of David armband). One year later, even these children could no longer qualify as Aryans and joined the ranks of the Jews.

Heartrending spectacles took place when the children became involved; some of them fainted while begging their fathers: "We want to die with you, we don't want to part from you." But Hitler's race laws were inexorable and merciless. Would these unfortunate women and children ever see their husbands and fathers again? It seemed likely they would not. Never before in the history of the Jewish community of Lvov had there been such a consensus among the rabbis as in those times. Separate courts were abolished, all differences between the Hasidim and the Mitnagdim (the fiercest opponents of the Hasidic movement), between the modern and the Orthodox, were put aside. All sat at the same table in complete harmony. One marriage register was used by the entire staff. Joint sessions were convened, presided over by the director of the Religious Affairs Department, Moshe Hirshfrung, a well-known Agudath activist and a prominent scholar. Everyone sensed that they were presiding over the last chapter of the history of the Lvov rabbinate. These last Mohicans decided therefore to depart from this world with dignity. And, in fact, not one of them survived. Rabbi Israel Leib Wolfsberg, Rabbi Moshe Elhanan Alter, Rabbi Moshe Aharonpreiss, and Rabbi Dr. Kalman Chameides died of typhus. Others were swallowed up by the mysterious, terror-inspiring Belzec, shrouded in mystery. Only I was left alive, like the messenger in the tragedy of Job: "And I only am escaped alone to tell thee." Shall I live to see the end of this horror? Only God knows.

This was, then, the structure of the religious community and its institutions. At first, only two departments functioned: Supplies and Labor. Months passed before other departments emerged and assumed their final form as described above. In the course of their expansion, the Judenrat institutions took over a number of buildings. The communal board occupied the main building at 2 Starotandetna Street. The second building was located at 12 Bernstein Street. The Housing Department was located at first in the building of the Vorstadt synagogue; later it moved to Stanislaw Street, to the former Kohn school. The Social Welfare Department together with the association for mutual assistance (YSA) were located in the Hadashim synagogue at Weglana Street.

The Judenrat inaugurated its activity by raising the infamous "contributions" (levies). This was supposed to be its gala show.

The German authorities imposed a levy of twenty million rubles on the Judenrat to be used for financing the reconstruction of the city after the damages of the siege. Why was it imposed on Jews, of all people? Were they the only residents of the city? What offense warranted such an exorbitant fine as punishment? Questions such as these were asked only in the first days of the occupation. Later the Jews grew used to not understanding anything and ceased asking questions altogether.

The levy caused great commotion among the Jews. They were stricken with fear at the prospect of not being able to raise such an enormous sum (the Germans gave us ten days to raise the money). However, the sense of duty manifested by the voluntary and extensive fund-raising drive among the Jewish masses, including the poorest sections of the community, dissipated all fears. Suits of clothing, expensive dresses, jewelry, and furniture were sold at half-price to raise money.

The news of the sale spread quickly among the peasants of the Lvov district. They began arriving in the city in droves. For the price of a cartload of vegetables, they dressed themselves like lords and took home expensive furniture. Poor Jews hurried to pay the fine. Those unable to raise cash gave cutlery, dishes, or silver candlesticks. Scores of Jewish women parted with their only valuable possession, their wedding rings, as an offering to the German Moloch.

There were some noteworthy displays of sympathy on the part of some Aryan citizens. Christian women came to the collection points to pay the fine in a demonstration of sympathy. Even two German officers appeared to show their displeasure with the orders of their superiors.

This fund-raising drive produced a great surplus, which the Judenrat set aside for future expenditures. Officials of the Judenrat scared the poor into believing that the levy had not yet been raised, thereby enabling them to relieve people of their last possessions. The Supplies Department could carry on with its work.

In the course of time the Jews became accustomed to the levies, so that the imposition of new ones failed to arouse interest or make an impression. The public was disabused of the hope that paying up would help in any way. No one brought a penny of his own will, so the Judenrat had to pay the fines through its own efforts.

The first levy had one beneficial effect. For two full weeks, as long as the fund-raising drive went on, no one harmed the Jews. They were not shot, and no one was brought to the Lecki prison. Once the lull was over, however, the Germans set upon Jews with redoubled energy.

One night Gestapo men surrounded Swieta Anna Street and arrested all the men on the pretext that someone had shot from there at the German barracks located near the Swieta Anna school. The next day all of those arrested were shot in Lecki prison.

The *Aktion* of collecting furniture was also launched with great energy. This time the Germans did not wait for the Supplies Department to complete the job and began themselves to seize furniture in Jewish homes. All a Christian landlord had to do was to inform the Germans that rich Jews lived in his building, their apartments filled with modern furniture and household utensils. Immediately a German with several carts would materialize at the door. The Jewish tenant was ordered to leave the apartment within half an hour and the German carted off all his belongings. If within the appointed half hour the victim attempted to remove something the German had taken a fancy to, he would end up with a crushed skull or a broken rib. The streets of Lvov at that time were full of wide-platform carts laden with Jewish possessions.

Forced Labor

In August 1941, the first attempts to set up forced labor camps in the environs of Lvov got under way. Needless to say, they bore only a faint resemblance to the Janowski camp set up at a later time. Compared to it they amounted to quite a modest venture.

At first the Gestapo appropriated a farm in the village of Sokolniki, not far from Lvov. Then Jews, mostly young people, were seized in Lvov to work on the farm. The Jewish Labor Department also supplied many workers to the farm. When the workers failed to return to their homes the next day, department officials asked the Gestapo official who had come to fetch another contingent of workers what had happened to those in the first group and why they had not come back home for the night. The Gestapo man provided an unsatisfactory answer, saying he had not come to argue but to fetch workers.

Later on the terrible secret came to light. Of the first contingent of workers, no one returned. The Germans set them to back-breaking work, then shot them and buried their bodies in a mass grave along the fence on the farm. Of the second batch, only the weak were shot. The strong remained. The Germans were particularly keen on preserving skilled workers whom they employed to reconstruct the burned farm buildings.

Gradually the village of Sokolniki became a mass labor camp. There is no doubt that it served as a laboratory for the terrible labor camps set up later in Lvov and its environs.

The battle against everything that Judaism holds sacred formed part and parcel of the larger war against the Jewish people itself. In keeping with an age-old Gentile practice, anti-Jewish disturbances usually involved the burning of synagogues and profanation of holy vessels and other religious articles. The battle plans of the Gestapo, conceived with proverbial German thoroughness, included an important section dealing with the burning of synagogues.

On a sunny summer day in August 1941, the Germans set fire to the Hekhal—a large municipal synagogue on Bujamow Street. The new Great Synagogue in the Bogdanowka district was also set ablaze. As the buildings were consumed by flames, guards were posted around them to prevent anyone from trying to extinguish the blaze or to salvage anything. Firemen, alerted the previous day, put in an appearance to prevent the fire from spreading to the neighboring buildings.

The burning synagogues presented a dreadful sight. Thousands of people stood by at a safe distance, looking on with indifference or a smirk. Jews steered clear of the streets nearby. Whoever had to pass through them skulked out like a thief with his eyes cast to the ground as if caught in a shameful act.

The next day the Germans set fire to the Sykstuski synagogue on Szajnuch Street where I had officiated as a rabbi from 1929. Together with the building, the Germans also planned to consign to the flames the cantor, David Peker, who lived with his family in the synagogue courtyard. Several days afterward the cantor told me his story.

One morning three Gestapo men showed up at his doorstep and demanded the synagogue keys. From outside they ordered him to open the door. Having entered the synagogue, they tore down the curtain of the Ark of the Law, threw it on his head, and told him to sing. As he sang they beat and kicked him.

Then one of them took a long rope from his knapsack. The three set on him, bound his hands, and then suspended him, head down, from the large chandelier hanging over the pulpit. They proceeded to swing him from wall to wall until he lost consciousness. Then they left a can of kerosene in the vestibule, locked the door, and departed.

All the while his eldest son watched the Germans from a hiding place in the women's gallery. As soon as the Gestapo men had gone, he ran quickly home and told his mother what had happened. Using a ladder he descended from the gallery to the synagogue, cut the rope, resuscitated his father with great effort, and brought him up to the first floor. From here he got him out through a side door and brought him home. They left the apartment the same day. At night the Germans set the synagogue on fire.

Cantor Peker outlived his synagogue. Exactly one year later, in the *Aktion* of August 1942, he was deported to Belzec together with his family. Foolish son, why did you save your father then? Wouldn't it have been better for him to die in the flames of the burning synagogue than in Belzec?

Emboldened by the German actions, the mobs of Lvov launched an onslaught against the remaining synagogues. They looted the fittings, tables, benches, lamps, tore down the roofs, and removed the window frames. Within a week, several synagogues were destroyed and reduced to rubble. Among others, the mob laid waste the architectural marvel of the Turi-Zahav synagogue on Blacharska Street, known as "the golden rose" (*di goldene roize*), one of the most beautiful gothic structures in Lvov, built by the Italian architect Paolo Romano in 1582.

Its insatiable demand for labor led the German government to institute labor duty within Germany itself and forced labor in all the occupied countries. Idleness was banned by law. Those not serving in the army were required to work in factories, to contribute to the economic war effort. Labor offices (*Arbeitsamt*) established for that purpose trapped everyone in an elaborate network of iron-clad rules and regulations. Woe to the man refusing to work. Even the nationals of the occupied countries were swept up in the dragnet of labor rules and enlisted in the production drive for the sake of a "New Europe." Whole villages east of Galicia were transferred to Germany to work in factories. At first, the young Ukrainian peasant let himself be enticed by the German ruse and would go willingly to Germany. Masses of such peasants came to Lvov and, before their train departed, these groups would raid the Jewish district to carry out heroic deeds: "We've played games with the Jews."

Once I had an opportunity to observe such a group, which took up its position below the Zamarstynow district bridge, waiting for victims. Tensely, with solemn, even festive expressions, they stood there waiting to commit their heinous deeds as if the fate of the Ukraine and an independent Ukrainian state depended on them. When these "heroes" left, the sidewalk was stained with blood.

The Jews, too, were swept up by the widening dragnet of the government labor offices, although it was evident that they were not to be taken to Germany but put to work in Lvov itself.

In early September, when the front lines had moved eastward a great distance from Lvov, various German military institutions serving the front installed themselves in the city and its environs. Their demand for forced labor knew no bounds. Private German companies working for the army also operated in the city. They, too, looked for workers.

In order to impress the Jews into the labor effort, to supervise the workers, and to prevent the shirking of labor duty, the authorities transferred the handling of labor matters from the Judenrat Labor Department to the jurisdiction of the newly established government office called *Arbeitsamt Lemberg—Judeneinsatz*. At first this institution was located in the building of the former Ukrainian school on Zamknieta Street and later in the school building across the Zamarstynow bridge.

The *Arbeitsamt-Judeneinsatz* was headed by Captain Weber, a degenerate and notorious drunkard, who for a whole year terrorized all Jews in general and the Lvov ghetto residents in particular. He had one good side, however: he could be bribed. The *Judeneinsatz* staff consisted of Jews only.

The German *Arbeitsamt* began by registering all Jewish residents of Lvov between the ages of sixteen and sixty. Each Jew was required to present a certificate from his place of work. This office had jurisdiction over all persons who had not yet found a place of work and therefore were liable to be sent to forced labor camps, which began functioning in late September. Such persons also could be put to work in Lvov itself.

Skilled and expert workers employed by various German firms in the city were furnished with a work card renewed by the *Judeneinsatz* each month. In those days every Jew dreamed of possessing such a card bearing Weber's signature. At that time the Germans still honored certificates issued by the Judenrat as equal in value to those of the German firms. Much worse was the situation of other groups, such as merchants or intelligentsia, who couldn't find work. It turned out that after the work registration, a Jew caught without a work card was free game. He could easily be dragged somewhere from which no one returned.

The demand for labor and work registration split the Jewish community into two categories: workers and nonworkers—the "productive," who could be put to work, and the unproductive, whom the German Reich labeled "asocial elements." In retrospect, this division turned out to be the bait of the trap that the Nazi state set for its Jewish captives and from which no one managed to escape. The rope was looped around the Jewish neck and the Germans pulled it slowly until the victim choked to death. The step-by-step liquidation of unproductive persons was beginning. Later it became the turn of the productive workers. Germany would be able to get along without the help of Jewish specialists.

For the time being the Germans refrained from putting the whole plan into effect. They contented themselves with laying the foundations for the future extermination. In the meantime, the Jews seized every opportunity to sneak into German factories as workers. One could acquire a work card and thereby a job by bribing the right people. People would make superhuman efforts, laboring from morning till night, and feel fortunate to get hold of Weber's signature. Jewish women who had never done hard work in their lives begged to be allowed to work as maids or laundresses in German homes and were overjoyed when given permission. The words of the prophet were thus fulfilled: "And you will sell yourselves to your enemy as servants and housemaids and they will want you not."

The Establishment of the Lvov Ghetto

When the High Holidays arrived, the remaining synagogues were under lock and key. No one dared pray in a synagogue and contravene the ban on public worship. Jews would assemble in private apartments in secret and pray, their hearts broken and spirits crushed.

As I write these lines, I can picture the scene in the house of my father-in-law on the eve of Yom Kippur during the Kol Nidre prayer. As was our custom on previous occasions, my wife, our little daughter, and I went to visit the elderly couple to wish them *Hatimah tovah* [a New Year's greeting-wish]. It was late. Large candles were burning, casting threatening shadows on the walls. My father-in-law stood wrapped in his prayer shawl, his white beard quivering under the ornamental fringe, his lips whispering *Tefilah zakah* (the confessional prayer said on the eve of the Day of Atonement). My mother-in-law was seated in the corner with tearful eyes. She wept as she read the lament of Kol Nidre from the Great Prayerbook. For the first time in their long, labor-filled lives, they were forced to pray at home on the eve of Yom Kippur. At that moment the door opened, letting in their three-year-old granddaughter, their daughter, and me. The old woman rose a bit, turning toward the granddaughter with a light smile on her face and suddenly, like a turbulent swollen river which bursts its dam, overflowing its banks, its mighty current sweeping everything on its way, the old woman burst into bitter, stirring, spasmatic tears. Her hands let go of the prayerbook and she fell on my neck. Then her daughter, husband, and son came from the next room. No word was said, no word of well-wishing was uttered. The heart, the Jewish heart with its emotional finesse, sensed that this time the daughter came not to be blessed but to part from them. This is how parents part from their children, brother from sister. This is how a family condemned to death says its farewell.

They did not live to see the next Yom Kippur. Their bones lie scattered somewhere in the pits of Belzec. No one cried on their grave.

The three-year-old granddaughter stood by, her face serious as if she already knew, as if she had understood the gravity of the moment. In a few months' time you shall part, little girl, from your parents on account of bad people. You will live among strangers, according to strange customs. You shall be called by a foreign name. Look well, my little girl, let this sight be etched deeply in your memory. Do not forget you are a daughter of Israel, the daughter of a holy people.

The summer of troubles and suffering passed. Then fall came with its cold, gloomy rains, bringing with it new troubles and new suffering. The problem of housing became acute. Every Jew knew that he would not be able to occupy his apartment much longer. Newspapers began publishing stories about the borders of the ghetto to be set up, as well as of important consultations on ways to cleanse the Aryan population of the Jewish plague. The Germans began expelling Jews not just from single apartments but from whole streets as well. The Gestapo stopped playing games with bureaucratic orders applying to individuals. In the morning, the SchuPo would make an appearance on the street, informing the Jews through janitors that they were required to evacuate their apartments within the next half hour. What can one remove from one's apartment in half an hour? Scores of Jews flocked to the Housing Department of the Judenrat. They would spend the night with their children outdoors, in attics, under staircases. From time to time prospective owners would appear at my apartment for a visit, examine it closely, ask me with a straight face whether it was dry, what its disadvantages were, as if I had posted a notice: "Apartment for rent." Its Jewish occupant ceased to be a factor in one's calculations.

I understood that sooner or later I would be driven out of my apartment and decided to embark on a search for another one. The judge of the Zniesienie district, Rabbi Hersh Rosenfeld, offered to share his apartment with my family. He lived at Jan Styk Street, which everyone expected would be included within the ghetto bounds. I didn't procrastinate much longer. I turned over the apartment to the first Pole who presented the "order," packed the remaining furniture, and, together with my parents-in-law, moved to Jan Styk Street. It was late September 1941.

On the day I moved into my new abode, I learned of an important development in the Jewish community. It turned out that the Germans had demanded a quota of five hundred young people for work in the new labor camps set up in Lvov and in other cities of the district. At that time labor camps were being set up in a number of villages in eastern Galicia: Kurowice, Jekatorov, Lecki, Winniki, and the notorious camp in Lvov itself, located at 123 Janowska Street; later it was to become famous throughout Poland.

The chairman of the Lvov Judenrat, Dr. Yosef Parnas, who realized the meaning of this demand, resolutely turned it down. His response was: "The Judenrat and its institutions had not been set up for the purpose of delivering our brethren to their death." This answer sealed his fate.

On the same day the Gestapo surrounded the main Judenrat building at Starotandetna Street and arrested nearly the entire staff, Parnas included. The young people were dispatched to the camps, whereas the detainees, Parnas among them, were shot in the prison at Lecki Street.

By demonstrating pride and determination, Dr. Yosef Parnas provided a shining example of the conduct of a representative of the Jewish community in times of crisis. Some time later this example was followed by the chairman of the Warsaw Judenrat, the engineer Adam Czerniakow. Parnas's successors in Lvov, however, failed to live up to his example. The story of Dr. Parnas's death is one of the few high points in the history of the Lvov ghetto.

The German commandant of Lvov replaced Dr. Parnas with his former deputy, Dr. Adolf Rotfeld. At the very first meeting he presided over, the Judenrat decided to acquiesce in the German request. Jewish policemen were dispatched to the streets immediately. Anyone caught without a work card was included in the labor camp quota. The new leaders of the Judenrat, however, went beyond what was required in this respect.

To assure swift execution of the German order, community wardens coerced the Judenrat staff into participating personally in seizures of people for forced labor. By nighttime two officials, lists in hand and escorted by a policeman, were dispatched to the streets. Their task was to take people from their beds and to take them to the detention center of the Jewish police.

Thus a man would be set against his brother, one Jew against another. In this fashion the Jewish police began discharging its contemptible, yet tragic, role in the Lvov ghetto.

The establishment of forced labor camps amounted to a prologue, a starting point for the events that were to unfold several days later.

On October 1, 1941, notices appeared on city walls proclaiming the establishment of a ghetto in Lvov. Since at that time some 100,000 Jews still lived in the city (over fifteen thousand had perished between July and October 1941), the designated ghetto site encompassed the entire Zamarstynow district, all of Zniesienie, part of Kleparow, and the former Jewish district known as the third district on both sides of Sloneczna Street. The Jews were ordered to evacuate their apartments and move to the ghetto within a fortnight. The city was divided into four sections. Every three days residents of one section were required to vacate their apartments. The Aryan residents of the would-be ghetto were allowed to remain until January 1942.

I cannot say that the decree about the establishment of the ghetto came as a surprise to us. Every Jew knew that sooner or later the same thing that had happened in all the large cities of the General Government was bound to take place in Lvov too. Nonetheless, the proclamation about establishment of the ghetto made a great impression on the Jewish population. Jews were seized by dread and panic. Thousands of people could be seen running to and fro in the narrow alleys of Zamarstynow, Zniesienie, and Kleparow. Everyone searched frantically for an apartment, going out of his way to secure a roof over the heads of his family. Those forced to evacuate their apartments forthwith succumbed to despair. With characteristic Jewish agitation, they would set upon small Jewish houses on the outskirts of the city, stop at the doorstep and ask: "Do you have an apartment for rent here?"

The Aryan residents of the designated ghetto area were not in a hurry to leave, despite the luxurious apartments waiting for them in the city. For each square meter to be vacated by them, they demanded astronomical sums. Suits of clothing, English fabric, astrakhan furs, bedroom furniture, gold dollars just flew in the air. Even the smallest space was measured and sold. Each pitiful hole was bought with gold.

If only the Jews were allowed to walk on the streets undisturbed as they searched for housing! But even this was denied them. The area swarmed with uniformed and plainclothes Gestapo agents who seized men for forced labor and searched for the sick and the elderly, the lame and the disabled. They would march them to a secret assembly point at the railroad bridge at Zrodlana Street.

The streets with the apartment that I had moved into recently was not included in the ghetto. Thus all my labor and torment were in vain. Together with thousands of other Jews I had to set out to look for a place to live. I looked for three consecutive days but found nothing. I almost succumbed to despair. Where should I go? To whom could I turn? Where could I find a corner for my wife's elderly parents and for my little girl? Only on the fourth day did my superhuman efforts bear fruit and I managed to find an apartment in Zniesienie. Located in a tiny house, the apartment consisted of one room and a kitchen, which we rented with another family. The house was located on the outskirts of Zniesienie, not far away from the swamp. Its damp walls hurt the eyes. There were no other choices and I felt lucky to have found anything. Eleven people lived in two tiny damp rooms. One could hardly move around the place as the floor was strewn with belongings.

As I was transferring my possessions from Jan Styk Street to Zniesienie, I ran into a Gestapo man. He wanted to see my papers. I showed him the Judenrat certificate. "This is good for nothing," he said and marched me to the assembly point at Zolkiewska Street where a group of Jews waited near a large wide-bed truck. They were guarded by another German, a young man with delicate features and blue, good eyes. The Gestapo man handed me over to him and set off in search for new victims.

To my horror I learned that this entire transport was scheduled to leave immediately for the Kurowice camp. Everything around me went dark and I nearly fainted.

I began pleading with the German to let me go, telling him that my family was waiting for me. I found myself here, I explained, by mistake, as my papers were in order. "Yes, yes," he replied, "all the others are here by mistake too." To his regret, he couldn't help us. An order is an order.

Suddenly, at a distance, I spotted my father-in-law. He was running down the street, skirting the streetcars and automobiles, his white beard flapping in the wind, his arms outstretched, his face bespeaking despair and heartrending grief. By God, an embodiment of the Jewish fate.

He ran up to me and fixed his agony-filled eyes on the face of the German. I noticed that something stirred in him. Who knows? Perhaps he was reminded of his old father left behind in the distant homeland. "What does he want?" he asked me. "This is my father-in-law," I said. "Well, quickly, get out of here!" I darted like an arrow to Jan Styk Street and my father-in-law returned to the cart and the belongings. No sooner had I evaded one danger, however, than I had to brace myself for fresh troubles.

Our janitor concluded that the events presented him with an exceptional opportunity. He figured he would be the greatest fool if he let such a moment slip away. To make the most of it, he demanded an expensive present from every Jew leaving his "abode." I gave him a suit of clothes. As this did not satisfy him he denounced me to the Gestapo: "The doctor on the second floor has hoarded a great deal of money and gold." This news was revealed to me by one of the Jewish tenants as I crossed my threshold. Like a hunted dog pursued by dogcatchers, I ran back to Zniesienie through short and narrow alleys I had never before used. Somehow I managed to reach my new apartment and for a long time I didn't dare venture outdoors.

At the time Jews were running about as if possessed, like drugged mice, along the filthy alleys of the ghetto, searching for a roof over their heads, a unique tragedy was unfolding under the railroad bridge at Zrodlana Street. Later it was called "the *Aktion* under the bridge."

What does "*Aktion*" mean? Taken literally, it means simply an action, an act by a group of people aimed at achieving some purpose, for example, a military action.

With us, an *Aktion* amounted to a brutal pogrom, plain and simple, and was followed by the dispatch of the captured victims to be killed by the Gestapo and the S.S. The final goal of an *Aktion* was to kill a certain number of Jews. This innocent-sounding, unsuspicious word implied horrific massacres and hair-raising atrocities. The *Aktionen* perpetrated by the Germans can only be compared to the heinous deeds of slave traders in the jungles of Africa in the nineteenth century, who would surround native villages and abduct all their inhabitants to sell into slavery.

The situation of these wretches, however, was better than that of the Jews under Nazi rule. The slaves could entertain some hope of gaining liberty one day, perhaps even of escaping. The Jew, on the other hand, was without hope; he could wait only for death.

The *Aktion* under the bridge was organized in an exemplary fashion. With the promulgation of the decree about the establishment of the ghetto, an order was issued that the traffic of Jews from the city to the ghetto be directed only through the Zrodlana Street bridge. All other streets and bridges were guarded by the Gestapo and the S.S., who drove away any Jew, directing him to the Zrodlana bridge. At the checkpoint on the bridge, every Jew and every Jewish cart were inspected closely. All valuables were confiscated and the owners were left with only rags. This was not, however, the primary objective of the *Aktion* under the bridge. All the elderly and disabled were separated and brought to a mysterious building to the right of the bridge, from which no one returned.

Much later I had an opportunity to speak with a number of reliable witnesses who succeeded in escaping from that hell. According to them, men and women were assembled separately in a large hall. The women were lined up in two columns. A bludgeon-wielding woman with the face of a witch positioned herself between the two columns. With enormous force she dealt blows to the right and left until the two columns fell on the floor, the women rolling in their own blood. The treatment accorded to the men was somewhat different—they were placed with their faces against the wall and shot one by one.

This, then, was the *Aktion* under the bridge.

One week later, when the Jews started to smuggle their elderly into the ghetto through the gardens of Kleparow and by other concealed pathways, the Gestapo launched an *Aktion* in private apartments. They went from house to house looking for the unfortunate ones, the defenseless elderly and disabled. Anyone caught without good, safe certificates fell into their hands. Thousands of old people committed suicide. Cyanide was to be found everywhere in those days. There was practically no Jewish house without this poison, our last resort.

The principal beneficiaries of the *Aktion* under the bridge were the Ukrainian policemen. Under the pretext of looking for the elderly, they would burst into Jewish homes at night, extorting large sums of money from the residents.

The *Aktion* under the bridge lasted nearly three months, until December 1941. According to the calculations of the Statistics Department, this particular *Aktion* swallowed up roughly ten thousand Jews. This figure apparently included, in addition to the elderly, the labor camp quotas and the suicides.

The painful problem of labor camp quotas grew more acute with each passing day. The Gestapo men were insatiable. They kept demanding more and more workers, while the Jewish policemen were slowly getting used to their role as man-catchers. They patrolled the ghetto streets every day, peeking into houses, looking for people out of work, the unfortunates without a work card in their possession. Some of those policemen, villains and criminals, became envious of their Ukrainian colleagues and turned this gruesome, contemptible occupation into a livelihood. The well-to-do could ransom themselves. Sad and bitter was the fate of a Jew with no money.

There were two camps within the city limits: at 123 Janowska Street and at 4 Czwartakow [Listopada] Street. Between twelve and fifteen people died in these two camps every day. The city of Lvov and the district of Galicia supplied the camp fodder. At first, the Germans would deliver the bodies to the Burial Department. Some of the bodies had been so beaten and battered that their facial features were barely recognizable. Some of them were shot, others died of hunger and other deprivations. Dreadful, paralyzing rumors about the Janowski camp began circulating in Lvov. At first no one believed them. One year later, when I found myself in this horrendous place, I realized that all the rumors about the Janowski camp were, unfortunately, true.

Meanwhile, the deadline for moving into the ghetto from the city expired. Shortly afterward, the city commandant issued a decree extending the deadline. The Jews who had not yet resettled in the ghetto were allowed to stay in their apartments. And, in fact, many did so until the great *Aktion* in August 1942.

The Gestapo could easily afford such generosity as it knew very well the fate in store for the Jews. Why then rush into setting up a ghetto, especially in view of the fact that at that time the Jewish population was still nearly 100,000 strong? Let the Jews wander from place to place and lose their property in the process. The ghetto borders would be changed several times anyway and in the end the Jews would leave no trace.

I continued to live in my new apartment in Zniesienie, in a small house on the outskirts of town. The fall passed, filled with trouble and torment, with gloomy, short cold days. Water trickled down our walls, as if rain were falling inside the apartment. It was difficult to stay indoors due to the foul air, the smell of rot, and the lack of a place to sit and concentrate. A dozen times a day we would hide in the cellar, trying to evade all kinds of man-catchers. We were too afraid to go out. "The sword without and terror within" (Deuteronomy 32:25)—impossible to stay home and impossible to go out.

At that time robbers began looting Jewish homes. Ordinary robbers took advantage of the prevailing lawlessness, as far as the Jews were concerned, by setting upon Jewish houses at night and despoiling anything still left. Jewish policemen armed only with rubber truncheons or plain sticks, stood by, unable to render assistance. The Jew became free game—anyone could hurt, kill, despoil him, and not even a dog would bark.

The first snows came and the year 1941 drew to a close.

The March Aktion

The *Aktion* under the bridge, which lasted until the last of December 1941, marked the end of the first stage in the battle waged by the Germans against the Jewish community of Lvov.

The first three months of 1942 passed rather uneventfully since, with the exception of a single *Aktion,* the so-called Fur *Aktion,* no noteworthy calamities were visited upon us. True, round-ups for forced labor camps continued and atrocities in the camp went on as before, but these involved personal tragedies which befell only isolated Jewish families. Nothing on a mass scale took place, as it did in Stanislawow, where thousands of Jews perished in the winter of 1941–42.

The winter of 1942 was unusually harsh. All roads were piled high with snow and the cold grew fiercer with each passing day. The vapor filling my tiny apartment in Zniesienie froze on the walls, creating a layer of ice more than an inch thick.

I still did not dare go out. My courageous wife went everywhere selling what was left of our possessions for a little food for our family. In January 1942, the Gestapo removed its guards from the bridges, thus bringing the *Aktion* under the bridge to an end. For the time being the Jews living in apartments in the city were not evacuated.

Only then did I summon enough courage to go out. I began frequenting the Religious Affairs Department, located in the former building of the Jewish community at 12 Bernstein Street, on a regular basis. Slowly other members of the rabbinate also appeared. By the end of January the rabbinate was fully staffed. As mentioned before, the Religious Affairs Department was headed by Moshe Hirshfrung, a well-known activist of Agudath Israel in Lvov, who also served as the rabbinate secretary. The Religious Affairs Department employed clerical staff furnished with Judenrat certificates. It goes without saying that this was a way of enabling a number of important unemployed figures to receive Judenrat certificates. Among them were two most well-mannered people, with whom I established friendly relations. One was the elderly Dr. Shmuel [Samuel] Rappaport from Zloczow, a scholar and a former Mizrachi activist. The second was Rabbi Hirshhorn of Biala, a native of Biala-Podolska, a noble soul of great sensitivity and sophisticated intelligence.

The Justice Department was located beneath us. As the aforementioned problem of divorces between Aryan women and Jewish men became more and more urgent, the Justice Department lent us a permanent legal adviser on these matters, Dr. Maurycy Allerhand, a former professor at Lvov University. He would confer with us for days on end and our long conversations are one of my most pleasant memories from those gloomy days. I never ceased to be amazed by the extraordinary liveliness of the quick mind, the multifaceted intelligence and erudition of this seventy-five-year-old gentleman. His talk amounted to an inexhaustible fount of wide-ranging knowledge of human affairs and gave evidence of his limitless familiarity with Jewish folklore. We used to talk for hours and I never grew tired of listening to him.

The Religious Affairs Department was entrusted with another important task. It had at its disposal a "collecting group"; its members went to the remaining study houses, gathering the Torah books, holy vessels, and other articles such as chandeliers, lamps, and books not yet despoiled by the Aryans. They were all stored in the spacious and warm cellars at 12 Bernstein Street. With successive additions this grew to be a one-of-a-kind museum that boasted rare holy books, as well as marvelous examples of applied crafts used in synagogues. Many exhibits exemplifying all that the Jews of Lvov had assembled with diligence and veneration over the past six hundred years of their history could be found there. Unfortunately, no trace remains now of this extraordinary collection. After eight months the Gestapo sent the whole collection to a raw materials processing facility where rare art objects and books of incalculable value lay in piles among heaps of rags and paper. At the gate of this facility, I once saw a collection of parchment sheets from Torah scrolls being loaded onto a truck by Jewish workers. As it is written: "The scrolls are consumed by flames and the letters fly up in the air."

As I noted earlier, the relative calm of the three winter months was broken once with the onset of the fur *Aktion*. In the middle of January a decree was issued requiring all Jews to turn over to the Germans all furs: coats, mantles, collars, and muffs. A piece of fur found in a Jewish home meant a death sentence for its owner. The Jews were also required to hand over wool sweaters, gloves, socks, ski suits, and ski gear.

The German army had its first taste of the bitter Russian cold so the fuehrer decided to do what he could to keep his faithful soldiers warm. Although the furs and sweaters were needed by the Jews, keeping the soldiers warm was all that mattered.

The fuehrer made a big mistake, however; only a minuscule proportion of the spoil yielded by the fur *Aktion* reached the German army. The most luxurious coats and astrakhan furs fell into the hands of the Gestapo; the soldiers continued to freeze. To assure the success of this *Aktion*, the Gestapo took ten Judenrat members as hostages and imprisoned them until the *Aktion* was completed.

This measure virtually guaranteed that the Judenrat institutions would plunge into fur collecting with great vigor and diligence. Within a short time, the Jewish residents parted with all the furs they owned. Everyone handed over his furs gladly, believing that perhaps he would thereby elude death.

After the fur *Aktion,* the ghetto enjoyed some calm. Jews were not harassed except by being forced to remove snow from all the streets. Only the foe within—the hunger, hardship, and cold—did not rest. Public kitchens swarmed with thousands of people waiting for a plate of watery soup, as for redemption. Terrible congestion facilitated the spread of disease. Typhus struck growing numbers of people.

In early February rumors began about a further constriction of the ghetto area. A Housing Department official revealed to me that the city commandant had said that Zniesienie must be cut off from the ghetto because of its many parks and its Aryan residents who could not be evacuated. This meant that we had to prepare for fresh wanderings, the third uprooting. I didn't waste much time thinking, and set out right away in search of another apartment. Soon enough I moved to 12 Zamarstynowska Street. I put up my wife's parents not far away on Balonowa Street. I hauled all my "great" possessions on a toy wagon within a few hours.

In my new apartment I learned the sad and terrible news of the fate of the Jewish community of Stanislawow. A young woman, the grand-daughter of my landlord, Yosef Duner, had just escaped from there. She had lived in Stanislawow before the war with her husband, a Jewish police officer, who had been shot.

She related to us the frightful atrocities perpetrated against the local Jews by the S.S. and Police Chief Krueger. Almost all Jews in the town were shot. Once the Stanislawow ghetto had been practically emptied of its residents, the Germans started bringing Jews in from the sur-rounding townships and villages until there were no Jews left in the entire district. The Jewish graveyard in Stanislawow turned into one huge mass grave. The woman had lived near the cemetery and she related to us a hair-raising scene she had observed from her window.

At the end of fall, several thousand Jews from the district townships were brought to the cemetery to be killed. The men of the Gestapo execution squad were dead drunk. As usual, such dramas unfolded in perfect order. The unfortunates waited for their death lined up in long columns. One unit kept order among the columns, while the other unit positioned itself behind the column on the edge of the pit and did the shooting. The victims fell straight into the pit. The notorious, well-rehearsed, and characteristic shot, aimed to the neck, which I observed later in the camp, worked instantly. The executioner would shoot into the victim's neck and the lifeless body would fall into the pit. However, as she related, on this occasion something went awry. The drunk Gestapo men lost control of the crowd and their shaking hands failed to aim accurately. Many Jews fell into the pits while still alive. Darkness had fallen. After the job was completed, the pit was covered with dirt.

The next day she noticed from her window that the mound of dirt stirred. Sometime afterward from the same window she saw her husband being killed together with a group of other Jews. He was shot for using his authority to get some Jews out of jail. She couldn't stay in Stanislawow any longer. She took her armband off, sneaked out of the ghetto, and fled to Lvov.

In February 1942, after I had moved out of Zniesienie, the second chairman of the Lvov Jewish community, Dr. Rotfeld, died after a prolonged illness. The city commandant appointed as his successor, his deputy, Dr. Landesberg. Most Jews greeted this appointment with satisfaction, as Landesberg was widely respected as a serious and honorable citizen. Many hoped that he would succeed in rooting out the corruption that had infested some of the Judenrat institutions. He was prevented, however, from taking advantage of the short lull following the *Aktion* under the bridge.

Shortly after Landesberg assumed this high office, rumors began to circulate in the ghetto that evacuation was imminent. In February, Jews had already been uprooted from a number of towns, from Rawa Ruska, for example. What was their destination? Where would they be settled? No one knew answers to these questions. Fantastic rumors and speculations as to their fate circulated in the ghetto; some said the uprooted had been sent to work in remote areas or settled in shacks in the swamps of Polesie. Others said that they were being deported to Germany to work in factories. A mystery surrounded these stories. There was something unclear about them, something wrong.

Toward the end of February 1942, everyone knew that the Jewish community in Lvov was to be swept by a new *Aktion*—"resettlement," or *Aussiedlung,* as the Germans called it. In itself, it didn't mean much. Ostensibly it suggested that a number of Jews had to be transferred from Lvov to some other place, since there were too many in the city. In early March, negotiations with the Gestapo commenced. How many Jews would be uprooted? The number was kept secret. Some said ten thousand; others, fifteen thousand. One thing was clear—the Gestapo told Landesberg that the Judenrat would carry out this *Aktion* using the Jewish police and that the evacuated Jews would be handed over to the Gestapo at the former building of the Sowiejski [Sobieski] school near the Zamarstynow bridge. Whose lot was going to be cast this time? Who was to be uprooted?

"Asocial elements," was the German reply.

"Asocial elements" could mean the underworld, thieves, robbers, or, in the broad sense of the term, the unemployed who do not contribute anything to the state. This could also refer, however, to individuals considered a burden to society, such as the poor, the alone, and the beggars.

Members of the underworld could be relied upon not to sit idly waiting for the Jewish police to come and hand them over to the Gestapo. They were smarter than that. Thus the lot would fall upon those out of work, i.e., those who did not have work cards, as well as the poor subsisting on a welfare allowance. As the Welfare Department had accurate lists of all welfare cases, the Judenrat decided to use this list first.

Early in March 1942, the welfare director, Dr. Kohn, was instructed to pass on to the Judenrat the addresses of all Jews supported by the community. The meaning of this became clearer when rumors began circulating that the purpose of the upcoming *Aktion* was not resettlement but simply death.

Rabbis at the Social Affairs Department became agitated and bitter. Is it possible? Can such an ignominious act be allowed to happen? Is one Jew entitled to send his coreligionist to death? All the more so when the case affects the poor, the luckless, and the innocent, whose only sin, penury, forced them to beg? Can such a thing be said to accord with Jewish law and morality?

After a brief and businesslike meeting, the board of rabbis resolved to dispatch a delegation to Dr. Landesberg regarding this matter. The delegation consisted of Rabbi Israel Wolfsberg, Rabbi Moshe Elhanan Alter, Rabbi Dr. Kalman Chameides, and me.

In the waiting room of the Judenrat at 2A Starotandetna Street we found a large number of people waiting for an interview with the chairman, Dr. Landesberg. German officers went in and out. The telephone was ringing constantly. The atmosphere was pervaded by nervousness and gloom. After half an hour Landesberg received us.

He looked pale and tired and his face showed visible traces of his terrible internal struggle. A man known for his excessive self-control, he looked nervous and absent-minded. We got straight down to business. We explained that in times of trial such as these we were duty bound to draw the attention of the leader of such a large Jewish community to the enormous responsibility associated with complying with the German orders. According to Jewish law and morality, he was to seek other ways. When our enemies come to us saying: "Bring one of you to us so that we may kill him. If not, we will kill you all"—it is better that all die and not one Jew be delivered to the enemy. This is what the Halakah rules.

We could see we touched a raw nerve. He turned angry and burst out: "You gentlemen appear to believe we live in prewar times and you come to the chairman of a religious *kehilla*. Let me tell you, the times have changed completely. We are no longer a religious community, but an instrument to carry out the orders of the Gestapo. And anyone who opposes the Gestapo. . . ."

The chairman did not finish the sentence, but we understood the implication. He was not willing to antagonize the Gestapo and risk his life. Such behavior could be understood in an individual, perhaps, but was hardly excusable in the case of the chief representative of a large Jewish community. True, the times had changed, but the law of the Torah, the morality and its foundations, remained intact and unaltered.

It is not for me to evaluate Dr. Landesberg's actions. All I am required to do is to tell the story as accurately as I can, in an objective manner. History will pass judgment as it sees fit.*

The *Aktion* commenced two weeks before Passover. The Judenrat mobilized Jewish policemen to assist in the job and see to it that no improprieties occurred. It turned out that, in fact, the *Aktion* began with uprooting the poorest Jews, those whose names appeared on the roster of the welfare cases. After several days these lists of names were no longer consulted; anyone caught without a work card was simply seized on the street. Every night the Sobieski school building was filled with luckless victims. After several days, when the building was packed, the Gestapo transferred them to the railroad station. They were loaded onto cars and the train departed. To where? For the time being, no one knew its destination.

The *Aktion* had been going on for a week, but the Gestapo was unsatisfied with the work of the Jewish policemen. The policemen were too lenient toward the Jews and brought in too few people. The

---

*See Appendix 2: An Account of the Rabbis' Meeting with Dr. Landesberg.

Germans decided therefore to complete the *Aktion* by themselves with the help of the Ukrainian policemen. The Jewish policemen were expendable.

First they seized old men with beards and sidelocks. Not even a work card could save a bearded Jew. Thus all those out of work were seized. During the *Aktion,* a Jewish commission operated in the Sobieski school building; it could request the release of a number of people it deemed productive to society. As this *Aktion* marked the beginning of future calamities, the Germans were interested in producing at least an outward impression that humane treatment was being accorded to the Jews. The chief of the German police in Lvov, Dr. Uhrlich, proclaimed that those scheduled for resettlement must be treated humanely.

I am at a loss to explain what this humane treatment consisted of; perhaps it was that it lacked the horrific spectacles with which the future *Aktion* was to abound.

A member of the Lvov rabbinate, Rabbi Anshel Schreiber, lost his life. He was a most gentle person, humble and respected. Seeing and hearing nothing, he was unaware of the rush of life around him, even though he was a great scholar of Torah, Hasidism, and kabala.

On Friday afternoon the *Aktion* reached its climax. No one could be seen on the street, every Jew out of work hid in his house. Rabbi Anshel Schreiber was with us all the time at the Religious Affairs Department. In the afternoon he announced serenely that he was going to the ritual bath. We tried to stop him, but to no avail. He simply could not forgo his wish to purify himself on Sabbath eve. As he was on his way, the Germans seized him and took him to the Sobieski school building. His Judenrat certificate was of no help to him; ten certificates were of no help to a Jew with a beard and sidelocks, dressed in a silk *kapoteh* [a traditional Jewish coat] girdled with a sash. The Judenrat made a special effort to save him, but to no avail. The Germans told us explicitly that they had been waiting for quite some time for such a singular specimen. They took pictures of him from every possible angle so that every German could delight at the picture of Rabbi Anshel Schreiber in the pages of *Der Sturmer.*

On Sunday morning Rabbi Anshel Schreiber dispatched a Jewish policeman to Dr. Landesberg. He was convinced that the Germans were mistakenly questioning the credibility of his certificate. He asked Landesberg to send someone to testify to the genuineness of his papers. Seidenfrau, a member of the Judenrat, came to him in the afternoon and told him the truth—it was not the document that did him in but his beard, sidelocks, Jewish appearance, and dress. "If this is so," he exclaimed with joy, "then blessed be His Name, for at least I know what I am dying for. And all the time I thought it was on account of this stupid certificate." He then proceeded to quote Rabbi Akiba (Berakhoth, 61:b): "All my life I have been concerned with the verse '[And you shall love the Lord your God] with all your soul, even when he takes your soul.' I said, when shall I be able to fulfill it, and now, when the opportunity came, shall I not fulfill it?" A sparkle appeared in his eyes and his face radiated joy. Is there a more beautiful moment in the life of a Jew than the moment he is told he will die for the Sanctification of the Name?

Rabbi Anshel Schreiber was a worthy successor of the Ashkenazi communities in the twelfth and thirteenth centuries, the time of the Crusades. Chroniclers of that time and composers of laments and confessional prayers tell us about the wondrous devotion displayed by whole Jewish communities who gladly gave their lives for their religion and faith. Rabbi Anshel Schreiber seemed to have come straight from that period. His abounding faith was pure and in the battle for his faith he knew no doubt or compromise, refusing to yield one iota. His outlook had the firmness of a rock without a trace of the inner rifts searing the souls of those steeped in the ways of Western culture. How great was your happiness, Rabbi Anshel Schreiber, how easy your death! Jews should envy you. Not many could say in their last moment: "I know what I am dying for." Most died because they happened to be born as Jews. For them, it must have been a terrible death.

The *Aktion,* later to be called the March *Aktion,* went on until Passover eve. On the final day the Germans did not honor any paper. A Jew had to go into hiding. The transport was scheduled to leave on the Seder night and the quota had not yet been reached. Everyone was subject to seizure. At night the *Aktion* reached its terrible climax. Jews gathered to observe the Passover Seder, believing that the murderers would not search for them at this particular time. They paid for this mistake with their lives.

On the first day of the Passover festival, we learned that Passover eve had turned out to be the last and blackest day of the March *Aktion.* Altogether, fifteen thousand Jews lost their lives in this *Aktion.*

With the liquidation of the assembly point at the Sobieski school building several days afterward, the Jews began inquiring about the destination of the victims of the last *Aktion.* As before, rumors and speculations abounded.

Slowly the bitter truth, the terrible secret, filtered back to us. Railroad workers who worked on that train revealed to us that the victims had been transported to Belzec, near Rawa Ruska.

What is Belzec?

Belzec is a small township located along the Lvov-Warsaw railroad, twenty kilometers from Rawa Ruska. In the woods some distance from the township, the Germans had erected many shacks and buildings, giving the impression of a camp. They surrounded the place with a high, impenetrable fence, reinforced with barbed wire. Off the main railroad they built a siding leading to the camp. Upon arrival at Belzec station, the train stopped and the engine driver and his assistants disembarked. A German driver climbed in and drove the train into the camp. On the same day he drove the empty train back to Belzec station. The Jews disappeared into the camp and were never seen again.

What befell the Jews taken there?

Not one Jew had managed to escape from Belzec at that time. Nor had an Aryan inhabitant of the area visited the place. Belzec remained shrouded in a thick and impenetrable veil of mystery. A terrible secret loomed over it. It could be revealed only with the departure of the Germans from Galicia. The only thing known at present is that Belzec is a mass grave of hundreds of thousands of Jewish victims. Buried there are Jews from France and Belgium, Czechoslovakia and Germany, nearly all the occupied countries in Europe. In the Janowski camp in Lvov there is a huge storage depot containing the clothes of Jews murdered at Belzec. Before being put to death they had been stripped naked. Among the clothes, suits were found with tags from nearly every European country. Some of the Western European Jews were brought to Belzec under the pretext of resettlement. German hypocrisy, the cold-blooded cynicism of the predator, knew no limits; the Jews were shown brochures of a flourishing Belzec colony with cinemas, theaters, hospitals, and schools.

How were the luckless victims killed?

Some say that electric current was used. According to others, the victims were killed with gas or hot steam. (Today we know from the only eyewitness who had succeeded in escaping from Belzec that they were gassed.) We do not know how the Germans disposed of the bodies, whether it was by burning them to ashes or by burying them in the ground. Burial does not seem plausible. How can millions be buried in such a small plot? Other rumors had it that the Germans extracted glycerine, soap, and other fats from the bodies. The fact is that clouds of black smoke could now and then be seen rising above Belzec and the stench was noticeable kilometers away.

From Aktion *to* Aktion

After the March *Aktion* the Jews of Lvov never knew peace again. Disasters came in rapid succession, one following close on the heels of the preceding one. It could be said that until June 1943 when the ghetto was finally liquidated, we lived in the midst of one large, continuous pogrom.

The first calamity after the March *Aktion* was the order issued by the *Arbeitsamt-Judeneinsatz* concerning the "A armband."

Rumors about this order had circulated even before the March *Aktion.* The *Arbeitsamt* director, Weber, requested an updated and detailed list of all Jewish workers. The registration carried out in the early fall of 1941 turned out to be unreliable. To assure that data on all Jewish workers would be strictly recorded, the *Arbeitsamt,* with the endorsement of the Gestapo, promulgated the following regulations:

All enterprises employing Jewish workers were obliged to furnish the *Arbeitsamt* with detailed rosters of their Jewish employees. The *Arbeitsamt* would then proceed to open a file for each worker, who would be furnished with a special paper called a *Melde-karte* (registration card) bearing the number of his file. Furthermore, each worker would be provided with a special armband, differing from the ordinary armband in that inside the Star of David a clearly visible letter "A" was sewn in red thread, together with the number of his *Melde-karte.* From that day on the Jew ceased to be a human being; instead, he became "*A Jude*" no. 1, 2, 3, and so on, or, in other words, a working Jew number so and so. In the future all permits received by Jewish workers would begin: "*Es wird hiermit bescheinigt, dass der "A" Jude Nr ... begibt sich nach ...* (It is hereby confirmed that the A Jew, number ... address ...)."

There was a special box on the *Melde-karte* for the use of the employing institution. The employer was to indicate there the length of time the bearer had been employed by him. Likewise, a discharge date could also be indicated in the box. An employer had to inform the *Arbeitsamt* that *A Jude* number so and so was dismissed from work. This marked the beginning of the tragedy of such an *A Jude.* He was no longer the master of his body, but a property of the *Arbeitsamt,* which could either send him to a camp or put him to work at some other location, as it saw fit. No German employer could use Jewish workers without the *Arbeitsamt* acting as intermediary. Promulgation of the A-armband regulation invalidated all other documents and certificates. Only the *Melde-karte* issued by the *Arbeitsamt* was valid.

The registration carried out by the *Arbeitsamt* in the fall of 1941 had already divided the Jewish residents into two categories: *Melde-karte* holders, either working or nonworking, and those who could not risk going out. The A armbands aggravated this situation even more. There was no longer any need to check papers. A glance on the armband was all it took.

The situation of the A-armband wearers was not so secure. No one could count on not being fired tomorrow. German enterprises used to dismiss Jewish workers for the slightest dereliction of duty and inform the *Arbeitsamt* immediately. The same night policemen would show up at the worker's door to transfer him to the camp on instructions of the *Arbeitsamt*.

The *Melde-karte* of the *Arbeitsamt* gave rise to another problem, the so-called household question. Each worker was entitled to demand protection for his wife and children. German enterprises supplied their workers with a document protecting their wives. Usually the Gestapo honored such documents. Now all these documents were abolished, as the *Arbeitsamt* took over the handling of these matters.

The authorities acted on the assumption that a worker's wife was in charge of the household of the entire family. One could ask for protection for one's mother or children who managed the household, or the worker's sister(s), when no mother or children were present. On the basis of her birth certificate, the *Arbeitsamt* furnished the wife with a *Melde-karte* bearing the number of her working husband, son, or brother. However, in the box for the use of the employer it carried the stamp of the *Arbeitsamt* saying: "This woman manages the household of the A-Jude number so and so." A woman holding such a *Melde-karte* was equal in status to her working husband. Before the August *Aktion* the Gestapo refrained from touching these women.

The household *Melde-karte* gave rise to a wave of marriages. Because a woman officially married to a worker could easily get hold of a household *Melde-karte,* many young women who had been engaged for a long time but had postponed their marriages in such hard times now decided to get married.

But not only young engaged women were suddenly overcome by a desire to get married. Fictitious marriages also began taking place. Men consented to marry women they had no intention of living with, solely to save their lives. Some of them were moved by pity, others by greed. In any event, the Religious Affairs Department was flooded with marriage applications.

Marriage officiants could not tell with certainty true marriages from fictitious ones. They were greatly confused. The institution of marriage was of cardinal importance in social life and a foundation of national existence. At the same time, however, rescuing a Jewish woman from death was tantamount to saving one soul of Israel ("For he who saves a soul of Israel, it is as if he saved the entire world"). The Talmud relates that in a time of hunger, Rabbi Tarfon, of the third generation of Tannaim, officiated as a priest at the marriage ceremonies of three hundred women to enable them to benefit from the Terumah (priestly tithe on produce) and thereby save their lives. In our case it was extremely hard to reach a unanimous and binding decision. Consequently each rabbi acted according to his conscience.

The Lvov *Arbeitsamt* continued to terrorize the Jewish community and the whole district before the August *Aktion*. Several Jewish Labor Department officials played a considerable role in these activities. The name of one of them deserves mention—a woman by the name of Shapiro, from Silesia, who exerted considerable influence on Weber.

Some fifty thousand A Jews were registered with the local Labor Office. Every one of them hoped that the A armband and the *Melde-karte* would save him from death. No one imagined that within a few months the *Melde-karte* would be abolished, the Labor Office dissolved, and its officials dispersed like mice, and that the Germans would come up with a new idea.

The period from the March *Aktion* to the August *Aktion* was replete with troubles and torments. Terrible anxiety prevailed everywhere and all Jews waited for something to happen. A sixth sense told us all that what we had gone through would be nothing compared to what awaited us in the future.

A series of small *Aktionen* unleashed against the Jewish community throughout the summer prepared the ground for the great disaster of August 1942. These *Aktionen* were the source of permanent tension which hardly left any breathing room.

On one such occasion a whole street was cordoned off, all apartments subjected to meticulous search, and whole families dragged to the prison at Lecki Street. On another occasion tenants of a building where a Jewish fugitive from the camp was hiding were shot at. Several times the Gestapo attempted to stage a real *Aktion* which lasted only half a day, but how many victims did it cost us?

In the course of one of these small *Aktionen,* the second religious judge of Lvov, Rabbi Simcha [Samuel?] Rappaport, lost his life. The German henchmen surprised him at his home in the morning when he was praying wrapped in a prayer shawl and wearing phylacteries. They dragged him outside and then chased him through the streets. He was beaten and forced to sing. I heard about this from people who, watching from their windows, saw him running. The spectacle was horrible. He ran, bleeding, his arms stretched wide. The prayer shawl which had slipped from his shoulders dragged behind him like a broken wing. He ran and wept: "Save us, for the sake of our God, save us!" The Germans marched behind him, hitting him with knouts, shouting: "Sing, Jude, sing!"

Conditions in the Janowski camp also deteriorated. Jewish policemen who had been stationed there related hair-raising stories. Names such as Willhaus, Rokita, Gebauer, Kolonko, and Blum sent shivers down the spine of every Jew in the ghetto. The public baths at Szpitalna Street had inscribed themselves in bloody letters on Jewish memory. The Germans would bring a large number of Jews there at the same time, usually at night. As the Jews stood naked under the sprinklers, the Germans opened fire from all sides into the thick crowd.

As the plague of typhoid struck every day at scores of victims in the camp, the camp commandant, *Lagerfuehrer* Willhaus, decided to carry out a thorough disinfection of the whole camp. This is how it was done: all Jewish prisoners handed over their clothes and remained naked. Then they were driven outside, assembled at the large camp yard, and the barracks were locked. They spent three days and nights outside for "disinfection." It was July, when days were dry and hot. During the day the sun beat on their heads mercilessly; there was no shade to hide in. Nearly everyone suffered sunstroke. At night they lowered their sick and burned bodies onto the bare ground, with nothing to cover them.

This is what the camp disinfection looked like. It came as no surprise that one-third of the prisoners did not survive it. This detail, however, did not bother the camp commandant. Disinfection was the main thing and the supply of Jews appeared endless.

To replenish the stock of prisoners, the Germans assembled several hundred Jewish policemen, took away their caps and other insignia of authority, dismissed them from the force, and led them to the camp.

For its part, the *Arbeitsamt* also made sure that a flow of unemployed

Jews would trickle slowly to the camp. The remainder were seized on the streets. Thus it happened that there was never a shortage of Jews in the camp. If for some reason the number of prisoners dwindled, the Germans would fill up the quota or even double it within a short period of time. Later the Judenrat ceased keeping records of those who died in the camp. The bodies were no longer dispatched to the Burial Department and instead were buried in the camp yard.

In the summer, before the August *Aktion,* hunger was ubiquitous in the ghetto. Despite the *Aktionen* and other forms of terror that claimed large numbers of victims, there were still tens of thousands of Jews in Lvov who had nothing to eat. Wages were ludicrously low. For all practical purposes the Jews worked for a work certificate. No belongings remained to be sold. The Germans had despoiled them, and, as it turned out, those deposited with Aryan neighbors were as good as gone. Only a handful of Aryan residents gave them back. Others maintained that the Gestapo had requisitioned them or told stories of theft. Often Gentiles simply kicked out a Jew who came to claim the belongings he had deposited with them. Jews no longer counted. What could these Jews live on? They simply died of hunger.

Gruesome, tragic scenes materialize before my eyes, heartrending scenes capable of squeezing tears out of a stone:

Early in the morning, between five and half past six, the whole Jewish district comes to life. All streets turn into rivers of people on their way to work. Haggard, emaciated by hunger, dressed in tatters, they move on. Everyone carries a knapsack or a pouch with bread. Ninety percent of this living matter streaming nervously through the ghetto streets and alleys have blue swollen faces and blue rings, swollen like pillows, around their eyes. Their bodies are simply bloated by hunger. Their daily diet consists of 70 grams of bread and a plate of thin, lukewarm, watery soup cooked by their wives at home. Having rested at night, been refreshed by a cup of black coffee sweetened with saccharine, and been nourished by their 70 grams of bread, their bodies appear more agile and movements quicker as they hurry to work. They must not to be late, God forbid, lest the *Arbeitsamt* learn of it. Between 7:00 A.M. and 5:00 P.M. no living soul can be seen on the streets, as if the ghetto has turned into a ghost town. At most, the lonely figure of a Judenrat official can be seen passing through, his one hand clutching a certificate and the other his soul; should Weber or Rokita catch him on the street during work time, no document in the world would save him. Occasionally one can spy an old man or woman forced by hunger to look outside for a crust of bread. Here and there, like a ghastly shadow afraid of daylight, a Jewish woman, a mother of children, scurries along in the direction of the only Jewish market, at Zamarstynowska Street, hoping against hope to buy some vegetables for her children.

At five in the evening the ghetto comes back to life. Slowly the streets fill up with workers returning home. Oh, Lord, how terrible are their countenances! Worn out and tormented, their eyes are almost invisible in their swollen faces. They pass slowly, dragging their feet, stopping to rest against the wall. Most terrible of all is the appearance of young boys. Sixteen, seventeen years old, skin and bones, skeletons wrapped up in bloated skin. And their faces! Whoever saw their eyes will never forget them, they will haunt him till the end of his days. "Why?" cry their pure, clear, innocent eyes. "Why? What have we done? Are we worse than other children in the whole world?"

I do not know whether the records of the Burial Department have been preserved. They would reveal to the world some interesting statistics. In August the director of the Burial Department, Dr. Reiss, showed me the list of the deceased: 50 percent of the Jews who had died before the August *Aktion* perished from hunger, 30 percent from typhoid, and 20 percent from other diseases.

The picture of the Lvov ghetto before the August *Aktion* would remain incomplete without mentioning the wanton, barbaric profanation of the Jewish cemetery. The Nazis were not content with tormenting the living Jews; they also vented their spleen upon the dead. A special labor battalion of Jewish workers from the camp was ordered to uproot and smash all the tombstones in the cemetery, to tear down the wall and reduce the requiem tabernacle to rubble. This ignominious work lasted for nearly a year. Slabs of prime marble were transported to Germany. Ordinary tombstones were used to pave the camp yard and the yards of various German institutions, or they were turned into gravel for paving roads.

In the library where I am writing these lines, I have found a small collection of papal bulls: *Die Papstlichen Bullen ueber die Blutbeschuldigung* (Papal bulls on the blood-libel, Munchen, 1900). In the bulls issued by Innocent IV on September 25, 1259, and by Gregory X on October 7, 1272, we read, inter alia, about a strict ban on profanation of Jewish graveyards: "*Ut nemo cimiterium Judeorum inutilitare vel iniuriere audebat*" (Let no one destroy or profane a Jewish cemetery). So it turns out that profanation of Jewish cemeteries is not a modern invention. Our history, however, had never seen anything like the cemetery profanation perpetrated by uniformed German thugs.

In July 1942, the first news reached Lvov about the terrible *Aktionen* in Krakow, Tarnow, Bochnia, Wieliczka, Jasna, and Krasna, which swept like a tidal wave over the entire western Galicia, pressing on toward Lvov. For the first time we heard about towns declared as "Judenrein" or, in simple words, towns whose Jewish residents had all been murdered. Stories circulated about endless trains packed with Jews pulling up daily at the Belzec station and disappearing into that mystery-veiled graveyard.

We realized that sooner or later Lvov's turn would come. Neither a *Melde-karte* nor an A armband would be of any help then; we had to look for other ways of rescue. It was then that the curtain was raised over the tragedy of the contemporary Marranos. The twentieth-century Marranos, however, fared much worse, as their circumstances set them apart from their Spanish predecessors.

In Spain, all a Jew had to do to save himself from death was to convert to Christianity. The Marranos, regarded as full-fledged Christians, enjoyed freedom of movement and no one harassed them. When the time was right to flee from Spain, they openly returned to the fold of Judaism. No state meted out punishment to them for that act.

Under Nazi rule, things were completely different. No apostasy could help. Every Jew, or apostate, or descendant of Jews down to the third generation was under the sentence of death, and all had to disappear from this world. A Jew seeking to save his life had to vanish and resurface as an Aryan or a "100% Aryan." This feat could be accomplished by means of forged documents called Aryan papers. Individuals lacking characteristically Jewish facial features and gesticulation and having a fluent command and unaccented pronunciation of Polish or Ukrainian arranged for themselves a set of forged documents: birth and marriage certificates, an old Polish passport, a special document testifying to the Aryan origins of its bearer, and a certificate of residence approved by the police. Having obtained this set of papers, the Jew would take off his armband, get on a train, ride to another city, and register himself as a resident on the basis of his new papers. He would then proceed to find a job and, provided no one recognized him or checked his real identity, wait until the danger passed.

Those Jews who stood no chance of passing as Aryans due to their characteristically Jewish appearance or accent, or because they wouldn't dare to live as Aryans, endeavored to hide in the houses of Aryan acquaintances for astronomical sums of money. They buried themselves alive behind walls to hide from German eyes.

I doubt whether anyone is capable of understanding the feelings of these phony Aryans or of those hiding in mouse burrows, waiting for the defeat of Hitler. A passing car, a stir, a suspicious noise sent shivers down their spines, their hearts would start thumping, their imaginations would go wild, and their limbs go numb. And, in fact, only a handful of these phony Aryans survived to the end of the war. All powers joined against the Jew. Everything betrayed him—his nervousness, his shaky knowledge of the catechism, his acquaintances and neighbors and, in most cases, those who hid him and then wanted to get rid of him and take his money. On the slightest suspicion he would be subjected to physical examination. Once the fact of circumcision was ascertained, the man was doomed and not even a dozen documents could save him.

A Jewish woman trying to hide had an easier time. After the liquidation of the ghetto many Jewish women sought to pass themselves off as *Volksdeutsche*. *Volksdeutsche* were mostly Poles whose paternal grandfather was German or who had a German relative. Such persons were allowed to demand for themselves the honorable title of *Volksdeutsche* and could then enjoy a nice supplement to their food rations. Jewish women decided to take advantage of this intricate genealogy and many of them succeeded in acting the part in a most accomplished manner.

Polish street folklore even produced a song about two *Volksdeutschen* whose true identity it purported to reveal:

Ojcze, ojcze
Ida sobie dwa Volksdeutsche
Ojcze, ojcze, co za wstyd
Jeden Polak, drugi Zyd.
[Father in heaven, see what's going on
Two Volksdeutschen walk along
Father in heaven, what a shame, these two:
One a Pole and one a Jew.]

In the course of time, however, even *Volksdeutsche* papers proved poor insurance. As I write these lines I have learned of a *Volksdeutsche* woman patient, seriously ill, who had been hospitalized for the last three months at a Ukrainian hospital on Piotr Skarga Street. Last night she was taken away by the Gestapo. It turned out she was Jewish.

Who informed on her? I don't know. What I do know was that evil tongues were at work every day. One heard countless stories about Jews being found out, about new victims. I am certain that without the assistance rendered by the local population, the Germans would have had no way of discovering so many Jews in hiding. Many of them would have survived if it weren't for the base denunciations by the Poles and the Ukrainians who had gotten accustomed to treating the Jew like a dog, like an animal hiding in the woods from the hunters.

The demand for Aryan papers gathered momentum in the summer of 1942. In Lvov it began shortly before the August *Aktion*, but in the General Government such documents had been in use for quite some time.

Small workshops turning out forged papers began to be established. People started trading in them.

Not every Jew, however, could afford the luxury of Aryan papers. Not everyone dared to take risks and not everyone had sufficient means at his disposal for that purpose. Most had to content themselves with simple hideouts within the ghetto.

Engineers, architects, and artisans put their brains and hands to work to construct hideouts in cellars and attics. They built double walls and hiding places where they couldn't be found except by denunciation.

Aryan chimney sweepers displayed a special malice in discovering such hideouts. Ostensibly engaged in searching for hidden smoke passages, they would come across hideouts, of which they informed the Gestapo.

In mid-July 1942, sudden rumors began that the *Melde-karte* were to be stamped by the Gestapo. A commission of Germans appeared at the Rohstoff-Erfassung works and demanded to see the list of all Jewish workers as well as their papers. Nearly every *Melde-karte* was stamped: "Der S.S. und Polizeifuehrer im Distrikt Galicin." Papers belonging to the elderly and disabled were not stamped. The Rohstoff works converted wreckage for military use. It occupied a prominent place among German enterprises employing Jews. Its German owner, Kremin, who made a fortune with the help of Jewish workers, had always protected them. Thus it was clear to everyone including the Rohstoff officials that a new *Aktion* was under way in which a *Melde-karte* not stamped by the S.S. would be of no value whatsoever.

Several days later, papers of workers at other locations were stamped by the Gestapo. There matters, however, took a different course. Important German institutions, such as the rail administration, Ostbahn, or Wehrmacht enterprises which employed large numbers of Jews, obtained nearly a full quota of stamped documents for their workers (excluding the elderly among them). In other places of work, 60 percent, half, or even fewer were stamped. The number of stamped documents depended on the mood of the members of the commission. Documents not stamped were confiscated and their holders transferred immediately to the camp.

All Jewish workers in the ghetto were seized by terror. Leaving for work in the morning, no one could be sure that his papers would be stamped so that he would be able to return home to his wife and children in the evening. In any event, all these rumors and guesses amounted to a preliminary phase before the upcoming *Aktion*.

In early August 1942 Governor General Dr. Frank arrived in Lvov. We knew that his visit did not bode well. All his previous visits came in advance of *Aktionen* against the Jews. To honor his presence, the Jews were forced to adorn the city, to sweep and clean up all the public squares. During his visit Jews were banned from the streets for three days.

After his departure, the *Arbeitsamt-Einsatz* was shut down and all its Jewish staff dismissed and dispersed; some of them fled. The artificial building which had been erected a year ago with such immense effort was demolished.

The abolition of the *Arbeitsamt* meant one thing: "We no longer need Jewish labor. Holders of the stamped *Melde-karte* will stay on, the rest will go to Belzec."

This was the last opportunity to do something. Every Jew undertook to look for ways of escape, at least for his children.

The Great Aktion *of August 1942:* *The Destruction of the Lvov Ghetto*

My colleague Rabbi Dr. Chameides and I decided to seek refuge with the Ukrainian Metropolitan Andrei Shepytskyi. There was nothing unusual about this; on more than one occasion Jews sought protection of senior church officials who often evinced understanding for their tragic situation.

We had already resolved, in line with the express wish of the Religious Affairs Department, to ask Metropolitan Sheptytskyi to hide several hundred Torah scrolls which had been left in the cellar at 12 Bernstein Street. On this occasion we also intended to submit a personal request—to be given refuge at his residence for the duration of the *Aktion*. The metropolitan had made a name for himself as a righteous man among the nations and we hoped he wouldn't turn us down.

We asked for an interview with the metropolitan through a Ukrainian priest, Dr. Gabriel Kostelnik, with whom I had become friends in the course of my many years of educational work in Lvov. The next day we set out in the direction of Jura Square to the metropolitan's palace.

A monk who had been apprised of the time of our arrival opened the door and escorted us to the antechamber on the first floor. The walls of the Jura Mountain palace left an odd impression on me. It seemed as if I had been suddenly lifted from a raging sea whose mighty gales threatened to overwhelm everything in their range, onto a quiet and peaceful island where every tree, every blade of grass, every flower seemed to ask in astonishment: "Is it really true that a terrible storm rages out on the sea?" The stillness prevailing among these walls was so soft we could hear clearly the beating of our hearts. After the wild, nervous tumult of the ghetto, I really thought we were walking on a different planet.

The metropolitan himself, a venerable, eighty-six-year-old man with a long white beard who for ten years had been paralyzed and confined to a wheelchair, made an even more powerful impression. He wasn't able to rise without help. His kind, deep-set eyes looked out above the frames of his glasses. It seemed that they expressed the promise of their owner to do everything possible on your behalf; loving his neighbor was the purpose of his life.

He asked us detailed questions about living conditions in the ghetto. Everything interested him. It was clear that the current Jewish tragedy moved him to the bottom of his soul. He told us of his attempts to plead the Jewish case with the German government. He had even lodged a strong protest with Himmler against employing Ukrainian youth as executioners of the Jews and inciting one people against another. He received a stiff and coarse response. The metropolitan continued to warn the Ukrainian people against evil and in his pastoral letters he endeavored to keep them away from hatred in general and from racial hatred in particular. He told us he was issuing a pastoral letter to the Ukrainian people and the clergy on the subject of mercy, in which he stated emphatically that in these times of trial one must pity not only the Ukrainians and the Christians, but everyone, regardless of his religion. The sin of murder occupied a prominent position in the letter. In the text printed by the organ of the archiepiscopacy "Lvivski Arkhieparkhialni Vidomosti" in August 1942, we read, inter alla: "It is with great pain and great anguish over the future of our people that I am obliged to say that in many of our flocks there are people whose soul and hands have been tainted by the innocent blood of their neighbors."

It goes without saying that he was prevented from stating clearly in his pastoral letter that the victims he had in mind were Jews. If he had, the Germans would have confiscated the newspaper immediately. In any event the archbishop did his utmost to alleviate the difficult situation of the Jews. Unfortunately, circumstances prevented him from accomplishing much. He would be glad to conceal the Torah scrolls, he said, on the condition that they would be brought to him by our people since it would be very difficult for him to send his emissaries to the ghetto. Furthermore, the Germans would have confiscated the scrolls on the way to the palace. As for saving our children, he stated his willingness to accept little boys and girls immediately, although it would be difficult to shelter circumcised boys. However, he promised to consult his brother, Abbot Kliment Sheptytskyi on this matter. He suggested we visit him the same day. As for ourselves, his home was open to us at all times. In times of peril we could count on his assistance despite the fact that sheltering Jews entailed deadly risk.

Half an hour later we were received by the metropolitan's brother, the archimandrite, i.e., head of all the monasteries of the Studite order.

Abbot Kliment Sheptytskyi, several years younger than his brother, looked and behaved like an ordinary Studite monk; his thin, ascetic face emerged from his white, narrow beard. This face bore no resemblance to the countenance of former Count Sheptytskyi. The abbot had devoted his life to the order of Studite monks, whose sole aspiration was to worship God and to treat men with benevolent kindness in all realms of life to the best of their abilities. First he gave me a letter to the head of convents, the Abbess Iosefa, who was to take my three-year-old daughter to her convent. He also promised to think about arrangements for other children and asked us to keep in touch with him.

This visit on August 14, 1942, settled my fate and the fate of a number of Jewish families.

On Saturday morning, August 15, 1942, we learned from reliable sources that the planned *Aktion* was to take place in the middle of next week, on Tuesday or Wednesday. Ukrainian policemen had been posted on all roads leading to Lvov. No Jew, even with an appropriate permit, could leave town. In several institutions the stamping of papers had already been completed. The German commission was in a hurry to finish its work. Everything indicated that these were the last days before the coming *Aktion*. Only members of the Judenrat staff still remained to have their papers stamped. They cherished an illusion that Landesberg would be able to exert an influence on the Germans to stamp at least a certain proportion of the papers of the Judenrat employees.

On Saturday morning every employee handed his *Melde-karte* to the Judenrat board and Landesberg took them all to Engels, the Gestapo chief in Lvov. He returned empty-handed. The Germans stamped only the papers of the members of the Judenrat and a few more belonging to employees of the Supplies and Sanitation departments. The papers of other workers were not returned. It was clear that in this *Aktion* the Germans would not honor documents of the Judenrat.

The time came to remove our daughter from the house. On Sunday morning, August 16, I set out on my way to the Studite convent situated far away from the ghetto, at 4 Obucz Street, a side alley in Liczakow. I was carrying with me the letter written by Abbot Kliment Sheptytskyi. It was a dangerous mission. With the exception of workers on their way to and from work, Jews were banned from walking on city streets. To walk the streets on Sunday was a daring act but I had no choice. I had to go. On Lyczakowska Street I ran into a frightened Jew who told me that farther down the street, about a fifteen-minute walk from there, several Germans were seizing all Jewish passersby. I decided to enter the nearest gate, take off my armband, and keep on walking as an Aryan. But to my dismay I found that someone was standing in every gate. When at last I spotted an empty gate I heard a coarse voice behind me shouting: "Hey, Jew, wait!" A heavy hand clasped my neck and dragged me into a courtyard where several Jews had been standing along a burnt wall, removing its bricks one by one. My captor was a civilian German with a jaundiced swollen face, his hand brandishing an iron rod. Before showing me what to do, he hit me several times on my shoulder with the bar. The blows took my breath away. Then he ordered me to pick up the bricks.

Within an hour the courtyard was filled with Jews, and the jaundiced German with the iron bar ordered them around. I began looking for an opening to get away. Across the wall, in the corner where I stacked up the bricks, I spied a loose board in the fence. I chose the moment when the German was preoccupied with something, tore down the board, and entered a garden. There I removed my armband and surveyed the surroundings. A narrow path led me to a side alley of the Liczakow district and on to the convent at Obucz Street.

Abbess Iosefa received me warmly and with kindness. She expressed her deep sympathy and understanding of the tragedy of the Jews. Only later, when she risked her life to save a large number of Jewish women and little girls, was I to realize that she spoke not out of politeness but from conviction.

We agreed that I would bring my daughter the next morning, August 17. I left reassured, believing the child would be in good hands. If my wife and I did not survive the Nazi hell, she would be sent to my brother in Jerusalem.

On my way back I didn't meet anyone. I returned home unmolested and told my wife about the visit to the convent. But "returned unmolested" in this context is but a figure of speech. My peace was shattered and my heart writhed in pain. I just couldn't watch my wife, who was unable to stop crying as she packed up the clothes of our little daughter. Tomorrow our child will leave us; who knows whether we shall see her again? Who will bring her up? What fate awaited her? I went out.

All around me I saw the same familiar dejection. Thousands of people were milling about on the ghetto streets. No one could sit still at home. People were saying farewell to each other on the street, quietly, simply, resigned to their fate, without theatrics. Simple words, laden with meaning, were heard everywhere: "Who knows, who knows, whether we shall be seeing each other again."

Sunday passed. We went to bed late at night; the child was to be sent in the morning to the convent. We were certain the *Aktion* would commence no earlier than Tuesday or Wednesday. The Gestapo, however, had other plans.

On Monday, August 17, at three o'clock in the morning, we were awakened by an uproar coming from Zamarstynowska Street. I opened the window and saw that the street was swarming with policemen—SchuPo, S.S., and the Ukrainians. They marched down Zamarstynowska Street to the right and disappeared in the side alleys. I understood that houses on the right side of Zamarstynowska Street would be the first to be hit. This meant that the *Aktion* was under way. It turned out I had labored in vain. I missed by one day.

Half an hour later we heard voices and shouts coming from the side alleys of Zamarstynow district. Now and then a shot was heard followed by a muffled broken scream. A number of people appeared at our door.

"Good dear people, let the fear of heaven be upon you, let us in! Perhaps we could hide here?" They told us that the districts of Zamarstynow and Kleparow were cut off from the ghetto and the city. All streets leading here were so closely guarded that not even a bird would be able to fly in or out.

What shall we do? Where shall we go? Where can we hide?

We must wake up the girl and dress her.

How can one wake up a three-year-old child at three in the morning? The girl started crying. People in the house began getting nervous, fearing her cry could be heard outside. Agitated and confused I drew up to her and slapped her behind. She responded by crying even louder. Oh, my dearest, sweet girl! Nearly two years have passed since that day. I have been through many ordeals, experienced many things, but I have not been able to forgive myself for slapping, even lightly, my little innocent lamb. I am sure I was not the only father to lose his temper that morning. Everywhere confused fathers stood helpless with their little children, just like me, asking one and the same question: "What shall I do? Where can we hide?"

The bathroom in our apartment could be entered through a small and low door. It was possible to place two closets along this wall to conceal the entrance completely. A person unfamiliar with the apartment would not conceive of the existence of an entrance that was perfectly camouflaged. The bathroom had enough space for twenty people, but by the time I made up my mind to enter it, there was no place left for my family.

I went down to the floor beneath us, where my colleague Dr. Reiser lived. His apartment too had a similar bathroom which was even better concealed. Moreover, his apartment was located on the side of the buiding and its entrance was not clearly visible from the front. The bathroom here was also full of people, but some space was found for my family. The owner locked us in. As the holder of a stamped *Melde-karte,* he was free to walk about his apartment.

Can anyone grasp what goes on in the mind of a human being buried in a hideout like this, dreading the visit by the Gestapo? Can anyone conceive the terror seizing more than twenty people pressed together in a small bathroom when they hear the sounds of hard, heavy tread characteristic of the S.S. thugs, coming from the courtyard and up the staircase. Can anyone picture the frozen silence, the fainting glances, the heartbeat of twenty people imprisoned in a tiny room, at the time the German opens the doors of the closet concealing the entrance to the bathroom?

Around eleven o'clock a knock was heard on the main door. I recognized the voice of my sister-in-law, who held a stamped *Melde-karte.* I moved the closet aside, left the hideout, and opened the apartment door to let her in.

With tears in her eyes she told me that at night the Germans had taken my wife's parents away and that she was now alone. But there was no time for emotions. My heart was frozen like ice. The Gestapo had just left the house, taking many Jews along with them. We must use the lull to send the child to the convent, before another gang showed up. Quickly I wrote a letter to a Polish acquaintance of mine, Professor Harhala. I described our situation and asked him to take our child to the Studite convent at Obucz Street. I also wrote a few words to Abbess Iosefa and added a separate farewell letter to our child in case we didn't survive the *Aktion*. My sister-in-law concealed the letters on her body, took the child with her, and set off.

Farewell my dear child! Shall I ever see you again? Your young mind was mature enough to realize that in a few moments we would part for a long, long time, perhaps forever. In the dark bathroom you clung to your mother and me, as if to console us and leave us with warm memories of you.

Dodging pursuers like a fugitive, my sister-in-law took the girl to Professor Harhala. He revealed himself to be a noble man and brought the child right away to the Studite convent.

We spent the whole day in the bathroom. The Gestapo called at the house several times during the day, but our hideout passed the test and no one discovered us.

Night came and the streets were a little safer. People started leaving their burrows. We learned of terrible things. There were many victims. All those discovered in hiding were shot on the spot. In our house, among other people, an old woman who nursed her typhoid-stricken grandson was taken away. They did not even let her dress the child. She wrapped him in a bed sheet and carried him in her arms. At that time her husband, an old ritual slaughterer, Meshulam Altstadt, was hiding and unable to help. Their stamped papers did not aid the elderly couple at all.

Not everyone waited passively for the Germans to come to take them away. Whole families committed suicide so as not to fall into German hands. People offered their entire property for cyanide pills.

The way the Germans handled that great Jewish enterprise, the so-called city workshops, which the city commandant had shares in and from whose output he reaped immense profit, was nothing short of odious hypocrisy. These workshops, manufacturing exclusively for the Wehrmacht, employed thousands of Jewish workers furnished with official certificates. In advance of the *Aktion* they had their papers stamped. When they arrived at work on the first day of the *Aktion* with their stamped *Melde-karte* in hand, they found that the whole place had been surrounded. The Germans then took all of them away. "How is that possible?" they kept asking. "Our papers have been stamped?!" "You have a blue stamp! The only valid papers are the ones stamped in red!" was the German reply.

Thus deceived, several thousand Jewish workers, holders of the *Melde-karte* with a blue stamp, were rounded up. Who could guess that the German knights would make a distinction between the blue stamps and the red ones?

The Jews who had been picked up in various places were assembled at the Ukrainian police station and from there marched to the Janowski camp. All day and night, flat, wide tram cars laden with Jews went to the Janowski camp. In the camp a selection was carried out—women, small children, the sick, and the aged were dispatched right away to the Kleparow railway station and from there to Belzec. The young and able-bodied remained in the Lvov camp or were sent to camps in the district.

I spent three days in the bathroom and each day was pervaded with the same paralyzing terror. We stayed in the hideout from dawn till night. At night we would go out to stretch our limbs. Our wives would cook some soup. The stomach refused to accustom itself to the *Aktion* and after three days of hiding in a bathroom, we were hungry. There was not a crust of bread or potatoes or vegetables in our apartment. I began thinking of doing something to get some food. It was clear that the *Aktion* would last a long time. Staying in our hideout without going out was tantamount to death by starvation. Seeking shelter at the metropolitan's residence was out of the question. The Jewish district remained sealed. There was only one way of getting out of the cage—to become a phony policeman. For the duration of the *Aktion* it was possible to get hold of a policeman's cap and a forged certificate from the Jewish police.

One of my neighbors was the deputy chief of the Jewish police, a former lawyer, Dr. R. On more than one occasion I had complained to him about the methods of his subordinates. On Thursday I went to his apartment, told him my story, and asked him to "sign me up" on the force for the duration of the *Aktion*. The next morning he brought me a cap, a yellow police armband, and a service book issued by the Jewish *Ordnungs-Dienst* stating that I was posted at the Second Commissariat at 132 Zamarstynowska Street as assistant policeman.

I could picture myself performing all sorts of jobs in my life, but I had never even dreamed of becoming a policeman. But I was far from treating the policeman's cap with disdain in times like these!

Thanks to the policeman's cap I became "unseen, yet seeing." It enabled me to observe things I wouldn't have seen otherwise and that would have remained unknown to the world forever had I stayed in my hideout.

On Thursday, August 20, before noon, I went out to the street for the first time and reported to the chief of the Second Commissariat.

The ghetto streets were empty. Not a living soul could be seen. Now and then a German or Ukrainian policeman passed by, escorting a small group of Jews to a collection point. Here and there shots rang out. The cart of the Burial Department went from house to house collecting the dead.

Nothing happened on the streets. All tragedies occurred within apartments, in cellars, attics, and compartments concealed by furniture.

From time to time a cry rose from the depths, shots were heard accompanied by the familiar sounds of heavy steps—then deadly silence again descended on the streets.

Bodies of a woman and a child were lying near the Second Commissariat. They had been shot dead the previous night. The Burial Department didn't have enough time to cart off so many bodies—the dead must wait their turn.

"Wepke did it," I was told by a young policeman, my former student. Wepke is a Gestapo man, a veritable predator, whose name instills terror in the hearts of ghetto residents. In the first two days of the *Aktion* he operated in the Zniesienie district. Since the previous day he had been active in the Second Commissariat. His specialty is to hunt down mothers with small children. He shoots the children before their mothers' eyes and he dispatches the mothers to the camp. This appears to give him great pleasure. "There is no point in sending children to Belzec," he is fond of saying.

The woman whose body lay there had not allowed Wepke to shoot her child and had set upon him with her nails. Wepke did her a favor and shot her along with the child.

On Friday, August 21, I asked for an order posting me to Starotandetna Street; I wanted to see for myself how the *Aktion* across the bridge was progressing.

Similar scenes were everywhere, the same destruction. As on our side of the bridge, there, too, not one Jew could be seen on the streets.

Instead, there were scores of Aryan residents who had come from the city to observe the Germans doing their work.

At Teodora Square, beside debris dating from the Polish pogrom of 1918, there was an outdoor collection station. Several hundred Jews stood there facing the wall, surrounded by S.S. men and Ukrainian policemen wielding long batons similar to those used by dogcatchers. At a distance, curious onlookers gathered in large and small groups. Among them were well-dressed men and women with mocking smiles on their faces, as if saying: "This is how it should be. The Jews are getting what they deserve!"

Utterly dejected, I left the third district and turned toward Kleparow. I wanted to inspect the neighborhood. No one so much as touched me; my cap gave me good protection.

The small buildings of Kleparow appeared orphaned. Their windows were smashed, their doors ripped out. The *Aktion* left its traces everywhere. Well-dressed fifteen- and sixteen-year-olds walked about. They had come from the city and were very busy helping the *Aktion* by searching for Jewish hideouts. I spotted one of them. Rushing out of a house, he shouted: "Mister, mister, over here, over here, *Jude!*" I realized that not so long ago I had seen this boy in the hallway of the Fifth Gymnasium, at Kuszewicz Street. He was a member of every possible student organization and had made a name for himself as a devout Catholic and ardent Polish patriot. In the future he no doubt will be a prominent member of every national academic society and will head the procession of national-religious youths on a pilgrimage to Czestochowa.

On Friday afternoon I learned that the Economy Department at Starotandetna Street would distribute a loaf of bread to each Judenrat official. For the last two weeks I have not received my full bread ration, so I set off for Starotandetna Street and stayed there for a while. On the way back I came across a Jewish policeman at Allembekow Street. Pale as a ghost, he blurted out: "A whole transport of Jews is being marched to the streetcar. Get out of here fast, or else they'll take you to escort them." I hid in one of the gates and through a narrow opening watched the procession. Several hundred Jews, mostly women, children, and the aged, trudged along in a column that filled the street. A number of S.S. men, Ukrainian policemen, and SchuPo walked beside them, long batons in hand, like shepherds around their flock. The utter helplessness of the Jews made the heavily armed guards look ludicrous. The Jews marched on slowly, step by step, the sound of their steps echoing in the deadly stillness of the street. Their faces were solemn and concentrated, as if absorbed by some important thought that united them all, and seemed to weave over them an invisible canopy of powerlessness. The deportees, who until recently had been nervous and distraught, trembling like fish caught in the net while waiting for the German henchmen to come, who had fainted time and again in their hideouts, who had wanted to live so much—now appeared utterly changed. Their faces bespoke quiet, meditative resignation, devoid of fear and theatrics. They had come to the simple conclusion: "We are Jews and therefore we must die. There is no alternative."

I was to observe the same expression, the same resignation, on the faces of my fellow camp inmates who, having undressed, waited naked for the S.S. man to reload his pistol and shoot them.

When it became clear that "my lot has been cast," the fear and maddening beating of the heart stopped; from then on every Jew waited for death quietly and with resignation.

Among the deportees bringing up the column's rear I recognized the familiar figure of a tall Jew with long, curly sidelocks and black piercing eyes. He carried a prayer shawl under his arm and a black sweater over his shoulders. It was Gedalche, the ritual slaughterer from Otynia. I had known him from my childhood, when the Russians evacuated all the Otynia Jews to Grzymalow. I had no idea how he had arrived in Lvov. Every Friday he came to me to ask for a donation. Once, when I asked him why he didn't go back to Otynia with other Jews, he said that he didn't want to spill blood anymore; he didn't want to work as a ritual slaughterer, fearing that after his death his soul would be reincarnated as a black crow. I couldn't get more out of him. Now, as he was drawing closer to my observation point, I noticed that his lips were moving and he muttered something. Was he reciting prayers to welcome the Sabbath?

The words with which Job's wife reproached him in his despair, pressed themselves on my lips: "Do you still retain your integrity?" Are you, Reb Gedalche, still a ritual slaughterer, still imbued with your flaming faith? If so, Hitler is taking away your body but not your soul.

I spent Saturday, August 22, at the commissariat. I didn't dare to go out on the streets again. Jews were brought in all the time. The Second Commissariat served as a transit point on the way to the general collection station. Jewish policemen were responsible with their necks for every prisoner. Sometimes it fell to the policemen to guard their own relatives and there was nothing they could do to help them.

On Sunday, August 23, the Gestapo men rested from their labors. After a week of hard work they deserved a proper day of rest. The Jewish district sighed with relief, but no one dared to appear on the street.

On Monday, August 24, I set off early for the Second Commissariat as usual. That Monday has etched itself deeply into my memory and I shall never be able to forget it.

That particular day was devoted to hunting down children. At 137 Zamarstynowska Street, opposite the building of the Jewish post office, a large truck pulled up. Eight young Germans climbed out. They wore elegant civilian clothes and their delicate facial features said these were pure Aryans. From looking at them, one would say they were not capable of killing a fly. They were followed by several Ukrainian policemen who took up positions near the post office. Then the Germans took to the streets.

I was unable to stand by and watch, as it would have made me appear suspect. When I passed by the post office a few hours later, however, I saw several dozen Jewish children sitting in the garden with the policemen guarding them. Their faces green, scared, and tearful, they huddled together. When one of them tried to get up, a policeman kicked him with his boot and forced him to remain seated.

I didn't see the children being loaded onto the truck. Later, the director of the Jewish post office told me that he had seen these refined German gentlemen throwing the children into the truck; they grabbed them by hands or feet and tossed them like so many sacks of potatoes. Although I was spared this scene, I had an opportunity to witness another in the afternoon.

Two children were playing on the street not far from the Zamarstynow commissariat. This is quite a common sight on the outskirts of Lvov. No one could have guessed that these were Jewish children. Nothing in their appearance, clothes, or the Polish suburban slang they spoke between themselves set them apart from their Aryan peers. At a distance two Ukrainian policemen could be seen slowly approaching. The children grew restless. They probably thought that the policemen had noticed them. Suddenly both children got up and started running. It is possible that the Ukrainian policemen wouldn't have paid any attention to the children who, as I said, looked like full-fledged Aryans.

By running away the children incriminated themselves. The policemen broke into pursuit but it was not easy to catch children who spent their days on the street. However, the policemen were not alone; Aryan residents rendered them wholehearted assistance. In less than a minute the whole of Zamarstynowska Street was filled with people. The old and young, big and small, all joined in pursuit of the little "criminals." You wretched people, how can your hearts contain so much evil?

One child succeeded in getting away. The other one was caught. The policemen handed him over for "safekeeping" to the Jewish policemen, took a receipt, and departed. The apprehended "criminal" was a ten- perhaps eleven-year-old boy with red hair and big, scared black eyes. His face twitched with mortal fear. He tried to shake himself loose from his captors and kept pleading tearfully: "Dear sir, please let me go back home to my mother." Everyone was deeply moved; tears welled up even in the eyes of the doomed Jews who waited for a truck to take them to the collection point. The child could not be pacified and had to be locked up in a cell with a barred window. This agitated him even more and he kept jumping up to the window, repeating his plea: "Dear sir, please let me go home!"

I spoke with the commissariat chief about releasing the child, but since the policemen had already issued a written receipt, this was out of the question. I walked up to the barred window and tried to pacify the boy. But what could I tell him? My heart was breaking with pain. The only thing I was able to learn from him was that his mother had sent both of them out to the street because they could no longer stand the cramped conditions in the hideout. Apparently she believed that they would be safer out on the street than in hiding.

Afterward the truck arrived and transferred all the Jews to the collection point. An S.S. man removed the boy from his cell and threw him on the truck. The boy kept repeating: "Dear sir, please let me go back home to my mother!" His words still echo in my memory.

On Wednesday, August 26, I had an opportunity for a close look at the collection point. In the evening, Jewish policemen were ordered to escort a Jewish court official to the commissariat of the Ukrainian police at Kazimierzowska Street. Among the escort I recognized my old friend Francuz, from our student days in Tarnopol. He persuaded me to join the escort. Since I knew that a large collection point for Jews was located near the Ukrainian police commissariat, I decided to take the opportunity to view it up close.

Gestapo men were bringing large and small groups of Jews in from all directions. The courtyard was packed with people; it looked like a marketplace. A long rope was stretched across the courtyard. On one side of it stood the Jews and on the other side their guards: Ukrainian policemen, Gestapo, and S.S. men. The place was quiet. No one said a word to his neighbor. On every face I observed the same expression of resignation that I had seen earlier on the faces of the Jews at Allembekow Street. After a while a fresh batch of Jews was shoved in with great noise and shouting by the Gestapo men, who appeared to be drunk. As they were being pushed to the other side of the rope, a baby's cry rose from one of the corners. It didn't stop. The baby cried even louder and its cry made everyone nervous, charging the atmosphere in the courtyard with tension.

I turned to see where the cry was coming from and saw a baby in diapers, swaddled in a shawl, laying on the staircase leading to a closed door. It was crying at the top of its lungs, but no one drew near to try to calm it. Several Germans approached the baby. A nervous officer started inquiring about its mother. No one could give him an answer. "For heaven's sake," the officer cried, "where is the mother of the baby?!"

It turned out that the mother, struck down by typhoid, had not been able to get up from her sickbed and had been shot on the spot. The baby had been given to a young girl who was taken away from the same building. The girl had apparently left the baby on the stairs and disappeared into the crowd.

With a heavy heart, my curiosity satisfied, I left the collection point.

On Thursday, August 27, the Jewish commissariat at Zamarstynowska Street went through some trying hours. Early in the morning a number of large trucks filled with Gestapo men pulled up at the Jewish hospital for contagious diseases located in the vicinity of the commissariat. The hospital wards were filled with typhoid victims. Also present were physicians on night duty, nurses, and other staff. The Gestapo men cordoned off the hospital building and then forced the physicians and staff to remove the patients and load them onto the waiting trucks. A number of Gestapo men burst into our commissariat and took several policemen on night duty to help with the job. Having finished evacuating the hospital, the Germans loaded the physicians, the hospital staff, and the policemen onto the last truck. All of them were driven straight to the railway station.

One of the Jewish policemen succeeded in jumping off the truck and escaping. He related to us the heartrending story of the evacuation. Unconscious patients were carried off in twos or threes on coarse canvas sheets. Patients who were still conscious begged the henchmen to shoot them right then and there to spare them the torments of the journey to Belzec. Their pleas proved fruitless.

That day the Germans evacuated two other hospitals, at Allembekow and Kuszewicz streets. All the patients were sent to Belzec. The hospital *Aktion* terrified the surviving Jews. Even after so many experiences, no one had expected such a display of cold-blooded and cruel cynicism. Later, when *Aktionen* against hospitals were carried out every month, no one was surprised anymore by these "heroic deeds" of the Germans.

On the same day, announcements were posted all over the city, signed by the notorious henchman, S.S. and police fuehrer, General Katzmann. He warned the Aryan residents of Lvov against sheltering Jews and threatened such persons with severe punishment. This indicated that not all hearts in Lvov were made of stone. It turned out that many Aryans displayed compassion and sympathy for the tormented Jews.

On Wednesday and Thursday, August 26 and 27, there was a lull in the *Aktion* until 2:00 p.m. The henchmen were busy "mopping up" small localities around Lvov such as Zuchowicze, Zimna Woda, and Zboisk [Zboiska?].

On Thursday at 2:00 p.m. the *Aktion* resumed with renewed fury. I was prevented from playing the policeman's part until the end. In one place the Gestapo uncovered a "phony policeman" and arrested him. The commissariat chief advised me to go home and immediately remove my policeman's cap.

My police career over, I reverted to the practices of other Jews by returning to the bathroom hideout.

On Friday, August 28, I learned that the Gestapo had arrested Dr. Landesberg in the Judenrat building at Starotandetna Street. No one knew the reason for the arrest.

On Saturday evening, August 29, the *Aktion* was over.

During its last two days, the *Aktion* raged primarily in the city's Aryan section where many Jews still lived. It should be noted that in nearly every tenement a committee was set up whose members visited each and every apartment to warn its residents against sheltering Jews.

On Sunday, August 30, announcements signed by Katzmann went up all over town proclaiming the new borders of the ghetto area. The so-called third district was amputated from the ghetto; it included streets on both sides of Zolkiewska and Sloneczna streets, the entire length of the right side of Zamarstynowska Street, Zniesienie, part of Kleparow, and the section of Zamarstynowska Street beginning with no. 105. Thus reduced, the ghetto was bounded on the east by a section of Zamarstynowska Street (its left side only) from the railway station to no. 105; south by the railway tracks from the Zamarstynow district bridge to Tetmajer Street; west by Tetmajer Street and north by alleys along the Zamarstynowska-Tetmajer section. The authorities immediately began to erect a fence along the new perimeter to separate the ghetto from the Aryan sections. In the future, no Jew would be allowed to leave the ghetto except for workers employed outside the ghetto or holders of a special permit. The announcement also said that "violators are subject to the death penalty."

It appears that Katzmann had in his possession a detailed register of all Lvov Jews. He also knew that the *Aktion* had swallowed over half the Jewish population and therefore was able to adjust the ghetto area to accommodate the surviving remnants.

In the course of the August *Aktion*, some sixty thousand Jews were exterminated. We were able to arrive at this figure later, on the basis of the number of bread-ration cards.

The Judenrat and its agencies had to move from their quarters at Starotandetna and Bernstein streets to a building that previously belonged to streetcar workers at Kuszewicz Street. At first only the Housing Department functioned; it was located at 5 Jakob Herman Street (the corner of Lokietek and Jakob Herman streets). The horrible scenes of November 1941 returned.

Thousands of Jews in search of housing were running to and fro along the narrow and filthy ghetto alleys. This time, however, the mood was different from a year ago. Children whose parents had been swept away by the *Aktion*, men whose wives and children had been lost, single persons whose families disappeared without a trace like a bough cut off from the tree trunk—all of them milled near the Housing Department, their faces masked with apathy.

The Housing Department, which had just begun organizing, did not function properly. At the same time, however, it must be noted that no basic prerequisites existed for a rational system of apartment allocation.

A number of divisions of the Housing Department operated outdoors in the courtyard. The ghetto area was very small and chaos prevailed everywhere. The apartment shortage made itself keenly felt once again. Several hyenas from the Housing Department again reared up their heads. People took up quarters in attics and cellars. Small orphaned children lay on the ground in the shadow of staircases. But these wretches no longer stirred anyone. The enormity of destruction left the survivors numb, their hearts turned to stone. Everyone passed by the hapless victims without blinking an eye.

By then every Jew saw death before his eyes. Everyone saw the fate the German plans intended for us. Even those who deluded themselves by believing that the Germans would refrain from exterminating Jewish workers had by now seen through the German designs. Everyone knew that the fate of the Jews was sealed and that whoever could not flee or hide in the nick of time would be tortured to death in the camp or be dispatched to Belzec.

In the Barracks and in Hiding

On a Wednesday or Thursday, sometime in September (I do not recall the exact date), several trucks carrying Gestapo men and Ukrainian policemen pulled up at Jakob Herman Street. They ringed the building housing the temporary offices of the Judenrat board, Jewish police, and Housing Department. At the same time all roads leading to Jakob Herman Street were cordoned off. At that time hundreds of Jews were crowded in the entrance to the Housing Department building and the courtyard, waiting for a decision on their housing applications.

The Gestapo men burst into the courtyard, removed the Jewish policemen found there, and assembled them next to one of the trucks under heavy guard. After detaining a large number of Jewish policemen, the Germans started erecting gallows by lowering ropes ending with nooses from the balconies facing Lokietek Street. A chair was placed under each noose and a Jewish policeman, hands bound, was led to each chair. The first noose, hanging from the balcony on the corner of Jakob Herman Street, remained "vacant" for the time being.

At this point, Katzmann's deputy, Engels, who personally directed the hanging of policemen, gave a signal. Dr. Landesberg was removed from a car and placed next to the first gallows. Housing Department officials, who at that time watched the scene from windows facing the street, later related that before he died, Landesberg bitterly reproached Engels saying: "So this is how the Germans are repaying me for having served them obediently like a dog." "And you shall die like a dog," replied Engels. Then the noose was slipped around his neck and the chair kicked aside. However, the rope snapped and the victim fell to the ground, hitting the sidewalk with his head.

According to an international custom, a sort of unwritten law honored by all nations, even barbarians, when the hanging rope snaps, the condemned man is freed. This custom however seems to have been unknown to the noble Germans. After a few minutes a strong, new rope was found which this time did not disappoint.

Thereupon the Germans started hanging the Jewish policemen. Within half an hour all Lokietek Street was adorned with hanging Jews.

As the hangmen were busy at their work, their comrades from the S.S. entered the courtyard, sprayed the Jews assembled there with machine gun fire, and departed, leaving behind them heaps of corpses.

Later the Germans said that the killings were carried out in reprisal for the murder of a German by a Jewish policeman. Ghetto residents did not believe it. The killings simply amounted to a public epilogue to the August *Aktion*.

The Jews acted with great restraint, gritted their teeth, and suffered all manner of restrictions and humiliations because everyone knew that the price exacted for one killed German would be dozens of Jewish victims. It was not out of cowardice that the Jews let themselves be oppressed and exposed their necks to the butcher's knife. On the contrary, one can only marvel at the sense of responsibility evident even among simple folk who under normal circumstances would never let an insult go by without a response. But now everyone understood the need to curb one's urge, for one individual's action endangered the lives of dozens of other Jews.

A member of the Stanislawow Judenrat who stayed in Lvov during the August *Aktion* related to me the following story:

At the Stanislawow cemetery where Krueger, the notorious killer, had shot countless Jews, scores of them were standing in a long line at the open grave, waiting for their death. In the back stood a young brave man, a butcher by profession, who openly incited the Jews to attack the Germans. "If we must die, at least I shall kill some Germans." One of the Jews replied: "Don't forget that there are still several thousand Jews left in town. Are you prepared to have them on your conscience?" The young man lowered his head, gritted his teeth, and waited patiently for his death. No, this was not an act of cowardice. These were heroic acts which we must honor, bowing our heads before them in respect.

Only toward the end, when the Jews lost all hope, when they realized that nothing would save them from certain death, did their patience become exhausted. Then we heard more often about single acts of vengeance against the Gestapo. At the end an open battle broke out. This is what happened in Lvov, as well as in Warsaw.

A long time passed after Dr. Landesberg's death before the Judenrat got reorganized. All Jewish residents succumbed to numbing apathy. Everyone saw that life such as this had no meaning whatsoever. No one was at rest. For several weeks the Judenrat functioned without a chairman; under the prevailing conditions, no one was willing to assume the responsibility that went with the job. No one wanted to risk his life. Finally Dr. Ebersohn, the only one to survive the destruction of his whole family, was elected; he said that having lost his family he had nothing more to lose. The new Judenrat did not resemble the old one. The clerical staff was considerably reduced. The pre–August *Aktion* momentum had exhausted itself. Judenrat certificates no longer had any value despite the stamp of the S.S. Only Jewish policemen honored it.

After the August *Aktion* unleashed in Lvov, the turn came for other cities and towns in Galicia. Everything proceeded according to a plan, map, and timetable of operations. The Germans did not skip one single township. In their boundless hypocrisy and deviousness, they even activated Jewish policemen from Lvov in the *Aktionen* carried out in the area. Jewish policemen were forced to work hand-in-hand with the Gestapo in dispatching their brethren to their death. Jews from villages and small towns would be herded into a larger town and from there transported to Belzec en masse.

In the early hours of the morning, trains packed with Jews would pass through Lvov on their way to Belzec. As usual, the Jews traveled in sealed freight cars with holes boarded up. One or two Gestapo men armed with machine guns were positioned either in the passageway or on the roof, ready to shoot any Jew attempting to jump off the train. The armed guards, however, did not scare anyone. The captives would break open the windows and doors and jump off the speeding train. Many broke their legs, or were killed or shot by the guards. A few managed to reach a Jewish settlement, thereby at least postponing their death for some time. Most of the escapees, however, returned to Lvov. They would sneak noiselessly into the ghetto and blend in with the crowds. In the course of time they became quite numerous. They were nicknamed "jumpers." Later, jumping off the train bound for Belzec became commonplace and every Jew carried in his pocket a small tool to be used in breaking open the car door or in drilling a hole in the wall or the floor.

Many Jews who had jumped off the train—dead, dying, or alive— could always be spotted along the railway to Belzec; those alive wandered through the woods in search of a Jewish settlement. I knew people who fell into the hands of the Germans several times and who jumped off the train several times. Some jumped three or four times. Some peasants took pity on the jumpers, fed them, and showed them the way back to the city. Other peasants turned them over to the Ukrainian police or the Gestapo.

The High Holidays were drawing near. Dejected, their spirits crushed, Jews were assembling in secret minyanim to pour out their bitter complaints in a silent prayer to the Maker of the world. One might do well to give an account of the mood prevailing then among the ghetto Jews, which they expressed in their prayers. These were not prayers of submission, of beating one's breasts with lowered head. They were not the traditional confession: "We are the guiltiest of all peoples" and the great calamity has been visited on our heads because of our sins.

No, the Jews of Lvov were animated by a different spirit on the Day of Atonement of 1942—the spirit of protest. Prayers were sounded as a reproach: Master of the world, why? For what sins? For what offenses have you singled us out from all peoples? Are the Ukrainians, the Poles, the Germans better than we are? Are other nations' moral standards higher than ours?

This mood did not resemble anything that came down to us in all the chronicles or in all the lamentations of the period of the Crusades. Then the Jew beat his breast and confessed his sins. He believed that he did, in fact, deserve the great punishment. Therefore his sufferings were easier to bear and his death easier to reconcile. But nowadays the Jews lacked that simple faith, a faith pure, clear, and lucid. His torments therefore were of incomparably greater intensity and much more tragic than those of his ancestors in the darkness of the Middle Ages.

I myself once asked the Lord: Please do not give my old mother, who has seen the death of her children, into the hands of Hitler; let her die in her bed.

I read in the paper that my native township of Grzymalow was now "Judenrein" and that all Jewesses had been sent to Skalat. I understood that an *Aktion* there was imminent and that everyone would be sent to Belzec. I asked the Lord with all my might to spare my elderly mother and take her to Him before the *Aktion*. My prayer did not go unanswered. One month later I learned that several days before the *Aktion,* on the thirteenth of Tishre, 1942, at the age of eighty-six, my mother closed her eyes forever. She was buried in the same cemetery where her martyred sons had been buried. No one recited kaddish on her grave, no one shed a tear. Her widowed daughter-in-law, together with her orphaned grandchildren, were on their way to Skalat. They departed before the *Aktion*. Her only daughter and her sons, residents of Tarnopol, had long since disappeared in Belzec.

My dear beloved mother! You were not a woman of the world. You did not spend your days in coffee houses or playing bridge. Your labor-filled years passed slowly and monotonously in a small and remote town. Always haunted and worried, you brought up your children with great effort. Your world consisted of your husband and children. Who doesn't know the thorny path of a Jewish mother? And when the sun of your life began setting, not one of your children stood by you. Together with thousands of other Jewish mothers, you flung them at Hitler's feet, sacrificed them on the terror-inspiring bloody altar, unknown in a Jewish history abounding with martyrs.

At that time I parted from my wife. Furnished with a letter of recommendation written by the Abbot Kliment Sheptytskyi and forged Aryan papers, my wife set off for the abbess of the Studite convent where she was to stay for a while. In no way could I reconcile myself to the possibility that my daughter might live as an orphan. One of us, my wife or I, must stay alive. If not, it was a distinct possibility that my daughter would never know of her origins. These thoughts gave me no rest and therefore I decided to remove the mother of my child from the ghetto.

My wife joined hundreds of other Jewish men and women on a trail of tears as modern Marranos. Although I was alone now in the ghetto, I calmed down somewhat; should I fail to survive, my daughter would not grow up as an orphan. Her mother would live and give her support.

In order to be able to maintain contact with the Abbot Kliment Sheptytskyi, with the help of my acquaintances I obtained a pass issued by the well-known German firm LPG (furs and leather), which enabled me to leave the ghetto and stay in the city. The LPG coordinator assigned me to the leather factory at Grodecka Street as a tanner. Again, as in the days of my youth, I had to learn. The factory was a short walk away from Jura Square where greetings from my wife and daughter were conveyed to me on a regular basis.

The ghetto, however, was far from calm. Large and small *Aktionen* and the resulting tragedies occurred daily. One day all Jews working at the Wehrmacht enterprise HKP were taken away to the camp. On another occasion a number of houses of Jewish workers employed at various S.S. institutions were surrounded and their occupants rounded up. The workers, together with their wives and children, were taken outside the city to the sandy hills near the Jewish graveyard and shot. They were buried on the spot.

The sandy hill in Lvov called in Polish *Gora Piaskowa* (sand mountain) or simply *Piaski* (sands) played an important role in the martyrdom of Lvov Jewry.

Had these sands been miraculously endowed with the faculty of speech, they doubtless would have related countless Jewish tragedies that took place there. Next to Belzec, these sands served as the largest mass grave of the Jews of Lvov. Usually the Germans brought groups of 150 to 200 people there. The victims first dug their own graves. Then they were ordered to strip naked and were shot one by one. The phrase "you'll end in the sands" entered common parlance and was used by everyone in a casual fashion. Everyone knew that if not in Belzec, then they would perish there in the sands.

In early November, when the erection of the fence around the ghetto had been nearly completed, rumors sprang up about new *Aktionen*. Harbingers of these future *Aktionen* were identification badges marked either with the letter W or R.

A large German company, Schwarz and Co., which exclusively employed Jewish workers to manufacture underwear and uniforms for the Wehrmacht, issued its employees, in addition to the usual pass with an R identification badge, a square piece of white fabric with a large letter R embroidered on it in black thread and stamped by the S.S.

This badge, sewn by its owner on the left side of his chest, meant: "Do not touch me. I am privileged to work for the German 'Riestungskommando'!"

A similar badge, but emboidered with a letter W, was issued to Jews employed by various Wehrmacht companies.

From that point on, only Jews possessing the R or W badge could hope to survive the next *Aktion*. Others, who wore the ordinary Jewish identification badge, were doomed.

Since the R and W badges appeared only two days before the *Aktion*, everyone was taken by surprise. Not everyone took this new identification seriously. Not all enterprises employing Jews had received the new badges from the Gestapo. Most of the companies working for the Wehrmacht learned of the badges only when the *Aktion* was already in full swing. The Gestapo, of course, took this into consideration.

They burst into the ghetto and, feigning ignorance, repeated the same old refrain: "Only Jews working for our army will be tolerated. People who don't work, the asocial elements, must be uprooted from here."

The fence around the ghetto was nearly completed. Ukrainian policemen guarded the few openings that remained. Armed guards also patrolled the perimeter. One could leave the ghetto only through the main gate at Zrodlana Street, situated before the famous Zrodlana bridge, known to us from the *Aktion* under the bridge. Under the bridge, Gestapo men sat in automobiles, awaiting their prey.

Senior officers and their entourage, under whose patronage the *Aktion* took place, stood at the gate. The large square in front of the main gate was packed with Jewish workers, most of whom were still without the W badge although they had work certificates, who sought to pass through the gate and go to work.

The Gestapo men, who had been active in the ghetto since the early morning, pushed every Jew toward the gate, as they knew that without the W badge they would not be allowed outside. In this fashion the Gestapo deceived the Jews who knew nothing, lured them into the cage, and sent them to their deaths.

I myself was nearly swept up by the November *Aktion*. One cold, rainy, and gloomy November morning, I heard suspicious sounds rising up from the street. When I opened the window, one look was enough to ascertain that disaster had struck. My experienced eyes immediately took in the typical scenes of an *Aktion*. Immediately I warned my neighbors.

The apartment was packed with people pressed together like sardines. The housing shortage in the ghetto was unbearable; people lived in attics and cellars. Needless to say, under these conditions it was impossible for everyone to hide. Even during the August *Aktion* there were not enough hideouts for everyone. Now in November, with the increase in the number of tenants, the shortage of hiding places was still more acute.

Since our famous bathroom proved too small to contain so many occupants, we decided that it would serve as a hiding place only for women, children, and persons lacking any work card; the rest stayed in the apartment waiting for the angels of death to come. It turned out that only two of us owned the W and R badges; the rest had ordinary work cards.

At five o'clock in the morning we heard the familiar sounds of the heavy steps of the Gestapo men. The door was left ajar so that the "visitors" would not suspect us of hiding. My heart was thumping, my eyes were filled with fear, my knees were weak in the familiar pre-*Aktion* agony felt by everyone with every fiber of his body.

We are waiting. Master of the world, I commit my soul to you. Do with us what you will.

The door opens. Three Germans with fleshy faces, armed from head to foot, enter the apartment; they are followed by several pale Jewish policemen. After examining our papers they take all of us, with the exception of the owners of W and R badges, to the dark courtyard, where many Jews have already been assembled under the guard of Jewish policemen and one German. Our bathroom remained undiscovered.

On my way out of the apartment I observed a striking scene: a young woman, stricken with typhoid, lay in our kitchen. A small child was with her. Her husband had been incarcerated in the Janowski camp, leaving her alone with the child. She was unconscious and the child calmly played with her hair. Such idyllic scenes could be observed in practically every apartment in the ghetto. Typhoid did not spare anyone and under conditions of terrible congestion in the ghetto, the disease was to be expected. I was certain that presently one of those nameless tragedies would unfold, with the Germans, as was their habit, shooting the mother and her child on the spot.

To my astonishment, the expected did not take place. One of the Germans, an older man with the prominent belly of a beer guzzler, stood by the kitchen door. He shook his head sadly and looked at this familiar scene with eyes not devoid of pity. He did not let his comrades enter the kitchen, but instead closed the door and took us out of the apartment.

This was not the first time I saw such behavior on the part of a German. To me it meant that Nazism had failed to poison the entire nation down to the last German. Not everyone was infected. The older generation proved to be more sensitive; at the time Hitler started disseminating his virulent theories, they were already grown men with beliefs and opinions of their own. Unfortunately, nearly all the Germans assigned to the ghetto were beasts in human disguise, plain and simple.

In the meantime the courtyard became packed with Jews. A few minutes passed but then my eyes became accustomed to the darkness. I was surrounded by people whose faces wore the same blank and somber expression of resignation. No one so much as uttered a sound. A gloomy silence enveloped us all. Everyone could hear his heart beating.

I made my way to the wall, leaned against it, and let myself be absorbed by my thoughts. What does one think about when facing a terrible, mysterious death in Belzec or, at best, incarceration in the Janowski camp? Is this the end? Does everything stop here?

I admit that I was hardly pressed to say "Blessed be the True Judge" for myself. Something in me resisted and rebelled against accepting this final sentence.

Flashbacks of my native township, my childhood, my parents, my murdered brothers, my studies, my public work in Lvov, my wife and daughter passed through my mind. How would my wife and daughter fare alone in an alien, cruel, and hostile world? Who would come to their help? To whom would they pour out their bitter complaints? Who would bring up my daughter? Who would guide her through the twisted paths of life?

I had always dreamed of happy days, when this tiny creature, my daughter, would become a grown woman, a person contributing her own share to human society, and I would argue with her, come to an understanding, exchange thoughts with her. And now? At that point a hand reached out to me and jolted me from my gloomy reflections.

"Doctor, I've been watching you for quite some time. Come here, stand by the door leading to the stairs. When the German turns away, I will open the door and you'll slip inside. Don't forget to remove your shoes right away so that your steps on the stairs won't be heard." Speaking to me was a former student of mine at the Fourth Gymnasium in Lvov, a gifted violinist named Rubin, who had graduated from the conservatory straight into the ranks of the Jewish police.

I do not know how it happened, but a few minutes later I was climbing stealthily, like a thief, shoes in hand, up the staircase. I knocked on the door of my apartment and the happy owner of a W badge opened it. In the kitchen the unconscious woman still lay on the floor. She was bleeding and her child, blissfully unaware, kept playing with her thick hair. My eyes met with his blue pure and smiling eyes. They were joyous, these child's eyes, radiant and full of vitality, despite the death lurking everywhere around us.

Oh, to live, to live no matter what! To live at any price!

All my senses, my entire being, was pervaded by one thought only—to live! In spite of Hitler, against the will of all who hate us—to live! Never before had I been so possessed by the will to live. Never before had I thought about it. Life had been something self-evident, like the ripening of grain, the blooming of flowers. I had known that the day would come and the flower would wilt, the reaper would come, sickle in hand, and cut down the standing corn. This is the way of the world created by God.

But to invade the field of corn like a wild boar, to uproot it so that no one would be able to enjoy it, to uproot the flowers and throw them into the garbage so that no one would enjoy their scent, their glorious colors—this was something I simply could not bring myself to accept.

As the persecution intensified, so did the bonds to life grow stronger until they became the sanctification of life. After the November *Aktion,* the life instinct grew in strength in the Lvov ghetto and the will to live became firm as a rock. Everyone, old and young, clung to one thought only: "To live! Oh, how strong is my will to live!" Every conversation between friends ended with these words. Our enemies doubtless would regard this phenomenon as a further vindication of their theory about our alleged commitment to material values. But our will to live was most natural, a necessity born out of the reality in which we lived. Each of us was like a deer surrounded by a pack of hungry wolves who does not give up hope as long as its legs can carry it, as long as its eyes are not clouded by the veil of darkness, as long as blood flows in its veins, and who keeps saying: "Perhaps I shall stay alive."

The November *Aktion,* which lasted a week, primarily swept up Jewish workers who had counted on their certificates and the stamped *Melde-karte* and had therefore not gone into hiding. However, there were many victims also among those who did hide. A small percentage of the captives arrived at the Janowski camp. The majority went straight to Belzec.

In order to reduce the number of jumpers, the Gestapo conceived of a devilish new idea: they took away the shoes and outer garments of the victims transported by train to the slaughter. The men were left with a shirt and trousers, while the women wore only a light dress or underskirt. Needless to say, jumping off a speeding train on a cold and rainy November day, barefoot and lightly dressed, was not an easy feat. But those able to jump did not let themselves be deterred, especially in view of the simple fact that they had nothing to lose. The number of jumpers increased with each passing day. A particularly high rate of jumping was recorded from packed trains making their way from small towns in eastern Galicia to Belzec. The jumpers would return to Lvov one by one, settle down in the ghetto, and gradually their names would enter the records of the ghetto population kept by the Statistic Department of the Judenrat. After November it proved impossible to ascertain how many of the Lvov Jews still remained alive. Ascertaining the number of Jews swallowed up by the November *Aktion* proved similarly difficult. It is estimated that fifteen thousand Jews lost their lives in this *Aktion.*

The November *Aktion* brought about yet another change in the life of the ghetto; first, the W badge, and second, "concentration" of working Jews together with their families in special tenements. This was called "barrackisation."

The A armbands, the *Melde-karte,* and even the W and R badges proved insufficient as a means of identifying all unemployed Jews subject to deportation to Belzec. After the November *Aktion,* forged W and R badges appeared in the ghetto, confusing the Gestapo and foiling their designs. It was impossible to check the papers of each and every ghetto resident. At first it was difficult to tell authentic and phony W badges apart. The Gestapo decided to solve this problem in a radical fashion. The ghetto was divided into two sections: A and B. Working Jews and their families were to live in section A, whereas the unemployed were to be concentrated in section B. Thus in the event of an *Aktion,* the Gestapo would not have to go to great lengths to pick out the victims—all residents of section B would go to Belzec.

German companies employing Jewish workers were ordered to concentrate all their employees in one place in the ghetto. A special directive was also issued to the Housing Department to allocate a number of tenements to each company according to the number of its Jewish employees. From then on these buildings were to be called the "barracks of company so-and-so" and the Jews living in them were called "barrack Jews of the so-and-so company." The so-called master Jews (*Ober-Juden*) were appointed as liaison officers between German companies and the Housing Department; they also served as the official representatives of the Jewish workers of a given company.

After the November *Aktion,* in addition to the barracks decree, the Gestapo also changed the working conditions and salaries of the Jewish workers. The German employer no longer paid wages to the Jews who were declared the "property" of S.S. Fuehrer General Katzmann. The German company was to transfer the Jewish workers' wages to the S.S. coffers every month. Every Jewish worker was remunerated for his labor with a daily ration of a plate of thin, watery soup, which no human being could possibly enjoy eating, 70 grams of bread, and a packet of coffee substitute, or something of the sort, once a month.

How different were the conditions in the Middle Ages! Then a German nobleman would impose heavy taxes on a Jew, whose status was that of *servus camerae* (servant of the royal chamber), and regard him as a source of income. At the same time, however, he at least extended his protection to the Jew in time of trouble and would even rescue him during a pogrom. And nowadays?

Every new German decree, every change, was aimed at torturing the

Jew, squeezing the last bit of marrow from his bones so that when finally nothing was left of him but an empty husk, he would be thrown like a piece of trash into the hellfire of Belzec.

The change of wages amounted to nothing more than a moral insult, another humiliation. The material loss did not amount to much. One way or another, the Jewish worker could not subsist on the few pennies he earned for his labor. If he happened to have nothing to sell, he and his family would have to die of starvation.

But "barrackisation" aroused great anger in the ghetto. In the first stage, all residents,—workers and nonworkers alike—of the buildings designated as "barracks" had to evacuate their apartments and move to the nonworkers' section of the ghetto. Then the workers and their families had to wait for the Housing Department and the *Ober-Juden* to divide up the ghetto into blocks belonging to various German industries. Only then were the workers allowed to take possession of their new quarters. In the course of these wanderings from one apartment to another, people lost the last of their possessions. Some moved in and out of an apartment three or four times before they found the right "barrack." The housing shortage became even more acute than in the aftermath of the August *Aktion*. The ghetto area was further reduced, whereas candidates for housing became more numerous. The municipality cut off the electricity and gas supply and in a number of buildings the water was also cut off.

This was the situation of the Lvov ghetto as it faced the winter of 1942–43.

2 ❧ THE JANOWSKI CAMP

Getting Acquainted with the Janowski Camp

With time, human beings can accommodate themselves to every conceivable adversity and the ghetto Jews were no exception. They set about in earnest fixing up living quarters in the "barracks" as if the German decree were the most natural thing in the world, as if its ultimate aim were not to exterminate them.

At the time that the officials of the Housing Department and the *Ober-Juden* were busy taking measurements of the ghetto and allocating buildings among various German companies, the Germans promulgated an ostensibly innocuous decree. But, as it turned out, this Gestapo order made the lives of many Jews intolerable and caused the deaths of others. Its meaning was simple: Beginning on November 17, 1942, no Jew was allowed to walk the streets alone. On their way to and from work, Jews were allowed to pass through the city in groups headed by an *Ober-Jude*. Walking on the sidewalk was forbidden, and Jews were required to walk in the street.

On the morning of November 17, I worked in the leather factory of the German LPG company. I had gotten hold of a phony W badge and set out for work every day. The Judenrat certificate had long since lost its value. The Religious Affairs Department had been dissolved. Only three of us remained of the entire rabbinate staff: the judge Rabbi Shlomke [Solomon] Rappaport, Dr. Kalman Chameides, and myself. Rabbi Shmuel [Samuel] Rappaport from Zielona Street, Rabbi Hersh Rosenfeld, and the rabbi of Zalozyce [Zalozycs], Nathan Nute Leiter, were killed in the August *Aktion*. Rabbi Israel Leib Wolfsberg, Rabbi Moshe Elhanan Alter and Rabbi Moshe Aharonpreiss died of typhoid. Rabbi Chameides had acquired a work certificate from the Rohstoff company and I continued to work at the LPG leather factory. At that time the concentration of Jewish workers in the barracks was due to begin. LPG employed over one thousand Jewish workers in various localities in the city who still had not been allocated barracks quarters and awaited the decision of the Housing Department. I had to move out of my current apartment at 21 Zamarstynowska Street and I took up quarters in a remote and filthy alley with the ludicrous [?] name Zamarsztynow, while waiting for a place at the LPG barracks. This was the fourth time I had moved.

The management of the leather factory asked me to take advantage of my numerous contacts at the Housing Department in order to solve the housing problem of company workers. At first I resisted the assignment, which required me to visit the ghetto, something I was not very keen to do. I also brought up as an argument the Gestapo decree issued the day before, but the management allayed my fears by furnishing me with a special pass. Jewish workers escorted me to the factory gate and I set out for the ghetto. How could I know what to expect on my way there?

It was an overcast, rainy, and gloomy November morning between nine and ten o'clock. Meditating on the saying "those sent on pious missions will meet no evil," I went down Grodecka Street, then Kazimierzowska Street, and turned toward Sloneczna Street, which the Jews called Slonce (sun) Street. On Sun Street I ran into a Jewish girl with a pale and frightened face. "Get out of here quick. Ukrainian policemen are seizing Jews on the streets."

"Even pass holders?" I asked.

"Yes, even people with the best of certificates."

I paid no heed to her warning and continued on my way to the ghetto. "Somehow I'll manage to elude them," I thought to myself. "After all, I am obliged to find housing for the Jewish workers from our factory."

Halfway down Sun Street an armed Ukrainian policeman darted out of one of the tenement gates.

"Kuda?" (Where are you going?), he asked.

I handed him my pass but he refused even to read it.

"I'll show you, you damned Jews, how to walk down the street without escort. Dogs are led on a leash!"

Within ten minutes, he had gathered eight Jews—five men and three women. Having lined us up in twos, he marched his captives to the Ukrainian police station at Kazimierzowska Street. The station yard was filled to overflowing with detained Jews. Every few minutes a policeman brought in a fresh batch of Jewish detainees. Later we were locked up in dark and filthy cells, men and women separately. Upon entering the cell each prisoner was served with a blow from a rifle butt so that he wouldn't forget, God forbid, where he was.

Once my eyes got used to the darkness, I was able to see our cell—eight meters long and six meters wide. It was packed with Jews, including the elderly, youths, and children. Some were seated on the floor or leaning against the wall, others were standing and talking quietly among themselves. Now and then the door opened and a policeman shoved in several more Jews. Gradually the congestion in the cell became so great it was difficult to breathe. What were they keeping us here for? What is going to happen to us? A man and his seven-year-old son stood next to me. The boy was trembling all over and kept asking his father: "Daddy, Daddy, when will we get to go home?"

The door stayed shut. Apparently the jailers realized that our cell had no more room. The whispered conversations slowly died down. The child next to me fell asleep. Everyone was absorbed in his own thoughts: What will happen to us? But no one dared to ask this question out loud.

Suddenly the door was thrown open revealing a Ukrainian police officer accompanied by two policemen: "Out! Everybody out! Line up in a column, five in a row!" Within a few moments we were lined up in a column, our bodies drawn taut like soldiers.

"Men over fifty, children under fifteen, step out of the column! Selection!"

Everybody understood the significance of this term. The young will in all likelihood be sent to a labor camp. The elderly and the children—disposed of in the junk yard.

The rigid, drawn up column collapsed. An S.S. man appeared.: "*Los! Los!* Faster!"

Heartrending scenes unfolded. Children started crying, refusing to part from their fathers. The Ukrainian policemen separated them by force. Commotion, cries, curses, blows, and more curses.

Half an hour later the inner yard of the police station at Kazimierzowska Street was cleansed of "unproductive" Jews. Only the young and healthy remained.

"From now on you are camp workers," said the S.S. man. "You'll live in the Janowski camp. If you behave well, you'll be better off than in the ghetto."

Good-bye freedom! Even though our existence in the ghetto was harsh and bitter, at least we could see some glimmer of freedom. Now I would be an inmate of the notorious Janowski forced labor camp.

A long column of several hundred people lined up in rows of five and, escorted by Ukrainian policemen under the command of the S.S. man, marched down Kazimierzowska and Janowska streets to the camp. As if to add insult to injury, the sun was shining brightly. People strolled about, women pushed baby prams and warmed themselves in the last rays of the autumn sun. The world went on as before. It refused to stop just because a few hundred Jews were led off to the Janowski camp.

At the end of Janowska Street, near the Kleparow railway station, the column halted in front of a large gate with a sign saying: "*Der S.S. und Polizei Fuehrer im Distrikt Galizieu. Zwangsgar beis Lager in Lemberg*" (S.S. and Police Fuehrer in the Galicia District. Lvov Forced Labor Camp). The S.S. man spoke to the guards and after a few minutes the gate—the hell gate—opened with a creak. Several hundred more victims stepped onto the camp's soil that was already drenched with the blood of martyrs.

On the way to the camp I remained in a state of shock and paralysis. The harsh sound of the gate slamming shut behind me jolted me back to my senses. I was a prisoner in the Janowski camp. Two different sayings entered my mind. One was from the Bible: "Take off your shoes from your feet, for the place whereon you stand is holy ground." The other was the one Dante had inscribed over the gates of his hell: "Abandon all hope, ye that enter this place."

The Janowski camp consisted of three sections. The first section was composed of garages, workshops, and offices; Jewish prisoners worked there for the camp management. This section also contained separate villas for the camp staff, the S.S. men, and the so-called askars—the host of traitors, mostly Ukrainians, soldiers of Vlasov, and Red Army defectors, all of whom placed themselves at the service of the Germans. At the center of the first section stood the villa of the camp commandant, *Obersturmfuehrer* Gustav Willhaus, the master of life and death in the Janowski camp.

The second section was the camp proper. In it, incarcerated behind barbed wire, were the doomed prisoners. Between seven and eight thousand Jews resided in the camp at all times. There was also a small number of non-Jewish prisoners sentenced for various offenses, who, after completing their sentences, were freed. They too were tortured but not killed. The prisoners lived (i.e., slept, since all their waking hours were devoted to work) in shacks on sleeping boards stacked up five or six on top of each other. In front there was a large roll-call yard.

The kitchen was located in the back, a gallows behind the kitchen, and latrines on the side. A lower ground led to a narrow opening in the barbed wire. The opening ended with a ball of barbed wire behind which there was a narrow gorge between two hills. All Lvovians knew these hills very well as "Kartumovka." Most of the executions were carried out in this gorge.

The policemen would march a group of Jews through the opening in the barbed wire fence to the gorge and shoot them. This narrow passage was nothing less than the last road of the Lvov Jews. Some of the victims were buried in the mass grave right then and there, whereas the bodies of others were burned.

Both the first and second sections were paved with chips of tomb-stones from the Lvov cemetery and with angular, sharp, unhewn cobble stones (in Polish *kocie lby*—cat heads). In particular, these sharp stones were purposely used to pave the path leading from the camp to the villa of camp commandant Willhaus; from time to time selections took place there. Guards would force the prisoners to run over the cat heads. The starved, weak, and exhausted Jews were forced to demonstrate their stamina by racing over these sharp stones. Only the healthy could finish the race without falling. Those who fell were removed to the "junk yard" (*na szmelc*) as it was called in the prisoners' slang.

The third section of the camp was called DAW (*Deutsche Auss-ristungs Werke*). In fact, it was nothing less than an industrial empire comprising factories and workshops belonging to the Goering concern. Later they would be called Hermann Goering Werke. The notorious murderer, *Haupsturmfuehrer* Gebauer, founder of the Janowski camp, was the ruler of the DAW empire. Over half of the Janowski camp prisoners and a large part of the ghetto labor force worked for DAW.

The three camp sections were separated from each other by a barbed-wire fence. The whole camp was surrounded with a double barbed-wire fence illuminated by electric light bulbs and search lights. Askars and S.S. men armed with machine guns were positioned day and night in the guard towers along the fence.

Like every good housemaster who looks after the household, the camp commandant, *Obersturmfuehrer* Willhaus, lived on the camp premises, near his enterprise. His villa was a small museum of sorts, a mansion of marvels filled with valuable objects pilfered from the Lvov ghetto. The man himself was a born killer and an excellent marksman in the bargain. He often engaged in live target practice from the balcony of his villa, the targets being prisoners walking about the camp yard.

One day, his daughter, with the original Nordic name Heike, celebrated her birthday. Her father, a man of refined sensibilities, wanted to entertain his little girl on her birthday; he took her by the hand, led her to the balcony, and pointed at the Jews walking in the camp yard. These were members of the "cripples brigade": people who barely stood on their legs, more dead than alive, who had been ejected from work crews on account of being unable to leave for work in the city. Willhaus picked them off one by one, shooting them like birds. Heike was beside herself with enthusiasm and joy, and kept clapping her hands. She seemed to take enormous pleasure in her father's skill.

Otilia, Willhaus's wife, was not a passive bystander either. Whenever a festive opportunity presented itself, such as a large *Aktion* in the ghetto, she too joined the operation with the help of a small hand gun that she owned. The devil himself must have been the matchmaker of this couple.

Willhaus had powerful protectors in the upper echelons. He was backed by S.S. and police fuehrer of the Galicia district, Major General Katzmann, who was very satisfied with his work and allowed him complete freedom of action.

The de facto ruler of the DAW, *Haupsturmfuehrer* Gebauer, was difficult to classify: Was he a man or the devil personified? Or, perhaps, a blend of the two? He was a tall officer, elegantly dressed, with the facial features of an aristocrat, black piercing eyes, affecting the manner of a movie star. He was also intelligent, his shrewdness bordering on slyness, and lacking any profession. He was the founder and organizer of the Janowski camp. Later, with the expansion of the camp and the appointment of Willhaus as its commandant, Gebauer became the master of the DAW. His specialty was strangulation. He knew exactly how to teach a lesson to a tired, broken Jewish prisoner who happened to fall asleep at work. He would stalk his prey slowly and silently like a cat, drawing near to his victim so as not to wake him up, God forbid. If the Jew was asleep on the ground, Gebauer would step on his neck with his elegant and polished boot and press it until the victim turned blue, stopped gasping for air, and expired. If the victim happened to fall asleep leaning over the worktable, Gebauer would remove the sweater from the worker's neck and strangle the man with his own sweater. If the Jewish worker did not have a sweater on his body, Gebauer would strangle him with his own aristocratic and manicured hands.

For lesser offenses, Gebauer would mete out punishment in the form of blows. If a Jewish prisoner stopped working for a moment to stretch his muscles or hauled on his back less than the quota of bricks pre-scribed by camp regulations, Gebauer would lunge at his prey like a hungry wolf, strip down his trousers, fling him on the ground and beat him with his leather knout. He kept on hitting until the victim stopped jerking, and Gebauer got tired.

In the future psychologists will perhaps undertake a study of the mind of a killer such as Gebauer. When he was strangling or hitting a victim, his face underwent a thorough transformation. The elegant, aristocratic-looking officer disappeared and in his place stood a sadistic murderer with a twitching, blood-thirsty face. The sight of a Jew rolling in his blood, being beaten to death, acted on him like a narcotic. The spasms and convulsions of the Jew he was strangling stimulated him, gave him pleasure, bringing him to the climax of his lust. But as soon as he stopped hitting or strangling, he immediately reverted to his former self, smoothed his uniform, put his gloves back on and, presto! the elegant, aristocratic-looking officer Gebauer stood before us—the perfect specimen of the "master race."

These were the two master henchmen of the camp. Apart from them, I remember very well a number of other sadists who have inscribed themselves on my mind forever. Thus I recall an S.S. man by the name of Blum, a man in his twenties at the most. He used to appear in the roll-call yard wielding a long whip with a noose at its end, like a cowboy out on a hunt for wild horses with a lasso. He then proceeded to select a victim from among the thousands of prisoners in the com-pound, the object of his game. Having found the right target—more often than not, an old, weak, exhausted Jew—he would slip the noose around his neck and start pulling until the Jew fell and died at his feet.

As a warehouse manager, Blum exercised control over the clothes, underwear, and shoes of the victims of Belzec and all eastern Galicia. Every day big cars, filled to overflowing, pulled up at his warehouse. By these cars we could tell which townships in eastern Galicia had become "Judenrein." He employed a great many Jewish workers. He had three chief storekeepers working for him: Schleicher, a former owner of a well-known carbonated drink factory in Lvov; the rabbi of Choloviev, who, if I remember correctly, was the son of the Busk rabbi, Babad; and Schreiber, an Agudath Israel party worker. During their stay in the camp the three men lost all human dignity. They devoted themselves wholeheartedly to worshipping the golden calf and finding a "fat suit" with diamonds or gold dollars sewn into it by its dead owner. Blum fattened himself through their efforts.

I also remember well an S.S. man by the name of Heinin: twenty-five years old, tall, with blue eyes, blond hair, and a red, congenial face. At first glance he appeared a nice man. But those who came into closer contact with him immediately recognized him for what he was.

Once I saw him guarding a group of Jews brought from the city with their hands bound. Even today I do not know why their hands were bound since it happened very seldom in the camp. Perhaps they were partisans, or were caught with forged papers in their possession. Wielding a submachine gun, Heinin walked around them like an animal stalking its prey. His face kept turning from red to blue and back to red. His nostrils flared, like a predator smelling blood. It was clear he was bursting with impatience, waiting for the moment he would be able to shoot his victims.

In my mind's eye I see the S.S. men who ruled over us during my stay in the camp: Willhaus's deputy Epler, Scheinbeck, Siler, Mansfeld, Wepke, Urmann, Kolonko, Heinisch, Grzymek, Brombauer.

It was Epler who received me in the reception office. He was a tall German officer, elegantly dressed, a long riding whip in his hand. He was standing in front of a group of several hundred Jewish women, counting them with a blow of the whip on the face. Among the women I recognized those who had been seized with us that morning. A detachment of askars took charge of the women counted by Epler and led them away. Several days later I learned that all of them were shot. At that time no camp for women existed.

Epler and Blum received the new arrivals who were brought in twos into the reception office. We were ordered to empty our pockets and lay everything we had on the table: documents, money, valuables. All I had was one hundred zloty and a work certificate.

"Where did you hide the money?" asked Blum.

I looked into his eyes and answered quietly that I had nothing except the one hundred zloty. This was enough to get Blum going. Blood rushed to his face, his nostrils flared, and presently I felt his knout dancing on my body. Most of the blows landed on my head. Blum calmed down only when he saw that my face turned brown and then blue and I was bleeding profusely from the nose and cheeks. He ripped off my W badge and handed me to a Jewish clerk who took down my personal data. Blum parted from me with a kick and threw me out.

Outside an askar took charge of me, adding me to a group of Jews who had already gone through the welcoming ceremony and had graduated into the ranks of prisoners of the forced labor camp in Lvov.

Although stunned, I managed to step into the row, but it took a long while before I came back to my senses. Someone gave me a piece of cotton wool with which I somehow stopped my nose from bleeding. Slowly my mind started working normally.

It was almost one o'clock in the afternoon. The sun disappeared once again behind the clouds, but there was no rain. Work stopped and the labor brigades started marching toward the kitchen to eat the midday meal.

Dressed in rags and tatters, their faces swollen with hunger, holding tin plates whose din resembled the clink-clank of charity boxes, the unskilled DAW workers marched in a long column toward the kitchen. They were followed by the brigades of skilled workers. The "cripples brigade" brought up the rear; it consisted of the human refuse from all other brigades, human shadows, ghosts. Only a few retained an erect posture. Most were bent, crooked, and broken human skeletons. They marched slowly, dragging their feet. From time to time two askars urged them on with sticks. In the meantime the last brigade had disappeared behind the shacks of the inner camp.

Three people walked out of the reception office. One carried a bucket and a brush; the second, a small knapsack; the third, a table and a chair. The one with the knapsack, apparently a brigade leader, wearing a yellow armband, ordered that the table and chair be placed next to us and addressed us as follows:

"As newly arrived prisoners you are required to have a haircut as prescribed by the camp regulations. From now on long hair or a crop of hair is forbidden. The barber standing here next to you will cut your hair down to the skin. Then the painter will paint red stripes on both sides of your trousers, as well as on the back of your jacket and your coat. It is forbidden to remove the paint which, by the way, is indelible. After the haircut each one of you will get a yellow triangular badge, a number sewn onto a piece of cloth, and a round disk with the same number on it to be worn around the neck. The yellow badge and the number will be sewn onto the left side of the front of your outer garment. After you are all trimmed and spruced up you will go to the baths. There also your clothes will be disinfected."

In the meantime the check in the reception office was over. More than four hundred beaten and bleeding people lined up in a column and waited for a "haircut."

At four o'clock we were all tidied up and ready to go to the baths. Before our departure Epler delivered a long speech:

"You should be happy you have found yourselves in the camp. In the camp there are truly free people, people who work, not like those parasites in the ghetto. Work makes you free. Of course you must abide by disciplinary regulations in force in the camp, work hard, be honest and clean. Also it is forbidden to escape from the camp. For every escaped prisoner, three others will be shot. Order must rule. At the same time, in the camp you are protected and you need not be afraid of *Aktionen* as in the ghetto. Here you get work, food, and lodgings."

We heard nice-sounding slogans, one of which was "work makes you free" (*Arbeit macht frei*); in short, we were in for an idyll.

After the long speech, four askars and two Jewish camp policemen escorted us to the baths at Szpitalna Street.

The baths at Szpitalna were well known to us all. It was the hellhole that during the summer had swallowed up dozens of victims. We went there, our hearts beating madly with fear. In the summer, policemen drove over a hundred people at a time to ten or twelve spigots spouting hot, almost boiling, water. No soap or towels were provided. Drunk S.S. men stood guard at the door, pistols drawn. People thronged as if gone mad. All wanted to stand at the wall, protected by a dam of naked bodies. When the tumult reached its peak, the S.S. men enforced peace by shooting into the naked mass.

We walked quickly toward the baths. Although we had not heard recently about such brutalities, one could never know. Perhaps today they will suddenly remember the days of Rokita?

Rokita, a *Volksdeutsche* from Upper Silesia, used to be a café player in Katowice. Today he is *Untersturmfuehrer der Waffen S.S.* This blood-thirsty beast never missed a single visit to the baths. He was the director of the devilish spectacle called "the Szpitalna Street baths."

We were lucky that in September 1942 Rokita was no longer in Lvov. He had established his own empire, his own camp in Tarnopol.

The spacious waiting hall of the Szpitalna Street baths was filled with light and merriment. Several askars were seated on the floor playing cards. Some of them stood at the main entrance, playing harmonica and singing sentimental Ukrainian songs, the *dumkas*. We were taken to the waiting hall and told to undress. Half of the new arrivals remained outside as there was not enough space in the baths for all of us. At this point we were subjected to a second search. The askars searched us on their own initiative and they did it much more thoroughly than the Germans in the reception office. First, the shoes; owners of good boots had to part with them and were given instead the worn-out boots of the askars. Our clothes too were subjected to meticulous search, which yielded quite a few diamonds and gold dollars that fell into the askars' hands.

This search, called "examination," lasted for over an hour; during all this time we stood naked, our teeth clattering. Then, without warning, one of them gave a signal and the askars set upon us with rifle butts and sticks, pushing the mass of two hundred people through the narrow opening inside the baths. While doing it they emboldened themselves by emitting wild, bizarre cries. The moans of the beaten people blended with the savage cries of their taskmasters. After several minutes all of us stood under the spigots that poured out boiling hot water which mocked our beaten and bleeding bodies and felt like salt on our wounds. As for the second group left outside, the askars contented themselves with a search only and did not take them inside.

This is what the misnamed "Szpitalna Street baths" amounted to.

At seven o'clock we returned to the camp. At the checkpoint booth we were counted and it turned out that two prisoners were missing; they apparently had managed to escape either from the baths or on our way back. We were stricken with fear. The escape meant that we would have to witness an execution at the start of our career in the camp. Whose lot was going to be cast this time?

The askars responsible for our numbers threw angry glances at us and marched us across the roll-call yard to Barracks no. 5 in the inner camp.

Barracks no. 5, the darkest and dirtiest of all the barracks in the camp, served as the living quarters for brigades of the simplest unskilled workers. The "Ostbahn brigade" occupied most of the space; it consisted of Jews working at the railway station in the most strenuous and filthy jobs, mainly in scrubbing locomotives. They were always covered with soot; their clothes were soiled beyond remedy. They were not allowed to wash themselves or launder their clothes, and they served as the favorite target of the mocking remarks of the S.S. men and Ukrainian railway policemen who regarded them as personifications of the "dirty Jew." During my stint in the camp, the "Ostbahn brigade" was the most wretched of all the labor brigades. It also supplied the largest quotas for executions.

Over the winter of 1943 I witnessed three executions of workers from this brigade. The most terrible of all took place on March 17, 1943, following the killing of an S.S. man by a Jew during work. The following morning during roll call, Willhaus avenged the death of the

German. He removed over thirty members of the "Ostbahn brigade" and shot them in front of us, one by one with his own hands. Altogether some two hundred Jews lost their lives in the camp and the ghetto that day.

In addition to the "Ostbahn brigade," there were five brigades of simple camp workers and one brigade employed in the city at construction. In my estimation about three hundred people lived in the barracks. A few light bulbs dimly illuminated the large rectangular room with three rows of six-story bunks. Prisoners walked in the passageways between the bunks as if inside long dark tunnels, offering for sale assorted goods: a slice of bread, a piece of herring, sugar, a small potato, or a small cup of coffee sweetened with sugar. There were also sellers of luxury goods: sausage, sweet bakery goods, chocolate, even liquor. For the most part the latter were young, alert, and resourceful men who took advantage of their work in the city to smuggle into the camp all sorts of merchandise. Now and then they peddled more dangerous merchandise such as underground broadsheets or Polish or Jewish underground newspapers which lifted our spirits and injected a little optimism into the hearts of the tormented and broken Jews.

Like the other barracks in the camp, Barracks no. 5 had its own orderlies and camp policemen in charge of order, sanitation, and security. The man in charge of all camp orderlies and policemen was Ormland, a shadowy character who made a fortune by collaborating with the German taskmasters and climbed to the summit of the camp hierarchy by reaching the rank of camp commandant.

The askars handed us over to Ormland and his underlings. They counted us again and led us to the barracks. As I have said, Barracks no. 5 was packed with prisoners. No one was prepared to share his narrow sleeping board. After prolonged bargaining, a camp policeman, my former student, helped me find a place on the sixth level in the middle row. The old-timers greeted us with indifference, sourness, and even dislike. A new transport meant more congestion in the barracks and less space on the already crowded sleeping boards. Slowly the barracks began to fill with human shadows—prisoners returning from work. Only a few evinced any interest in the new arrivals. Most of them went past us apathetically, their dull, glazed eyes meeting our nervous and restless glances. Completely worn out and exhausted by their day's work, they dropped on their filthy, lice-infested bunks and fell asleep instantly.

At 9:00 P.M. the few dim lights in the barracks went out. I was lying on my board but sleep did not come. Scenes of the past day kept appearing before my eyes, keeping me awake. This was the first day of my life in the camp, November 17, 1942. No one leaves this place alive. What will happen to my wife and daughter if they remain alive? Oh Master of the world, have you really made up Your mind to destroy Your people Israel? The *Aktionen,* the ways we are being exterminated surpass the most terrible curses of chastisement pronounced in the books of Deuteronomy and Leviticus.

I am lying on the sixth, top level of sleeping boards. A faint glow seeps inside near my bed—probably the light of projectors sweeping the camp now and then. My nervous hands feel the tin disc suspended from a string around my neck. It is stamped with a number, my "dog tag" (*Hunde Marke*). In the faint light filtering through the narrow porthole I see the digits making up my number: 2250. From now on I have no name, I am just a number, 2250. It tells me that up to November 17, 1942, thousands of Jews have passed through this camp and God only knows how many of them survived. But perhaps this number has yet another significance? According to kabala, numbers play as great a role in human life as do letters. Viewed in this way, the number 2250 is not all that simple. Its digits add up to nine: $2+2+5+0=9$. Number 9 possesses wondrous qualities. First, it is half of eighteen, or in Hebrew *hai,* meaning alive. Eighteen is $1+8$, 9 again. Talmudic sages say that "the stamp of the Holy One Blessed be He is *emeth* (truth)." The three Hebrew letters making up the word *emeth* (*aleph, mem, tav*) are 1, 40, and 400. Their sum is 441 ($1+40+400$). The three digits of this number also add up to 9 ($4+4+1$). I clung to my number like a drowning man clutching at a straw; to me it seemed a sign from heaven. Our Sages of Blessed Memory said: "Even when the blade of a sharp sword is on his neck, a man must remain merciful" (Tractate Berakhoth, 10). My situation as a prisoner in the Janowski camp was so hopeless that I could feel the blade of the sword on my neck. I didn't sleep a wink that night. I strained to the utmost not to give way to despair, turning over in my mind the phrase: "Even when the blade of a sharp sword. . . ." I decided to guard well my round disc with the number 9 meaning "alive."

At 4:30 A.M. the lights went on and the voice of the orderly resounded through the barracks: "Rise up Jews, rise up you camp dwellers, rise up you pissers, rise up to work." His voice was sorrowful, half cry, half laughter. The comical chant called to mind the chant of a synagogue beadle waking people up for Selikhoth. In short, it amounted to a tragicomical parody. Later I learned that in fact his father served as a synagogue beadle in a township in eastern Galicia. He repeated his wake-up call in the same voice every day.

All at once the barracks stirred with life. Drowsy but a bit rested, the prisoners hurriedly hauled themselves off the sleeping boards. The race to the latrines and baths commenced. Long lines quickly formed at both establishments; people were in a hurry to get rid of unnecessary burdens. To make the life of the prisoners as miserable as possible, both the latrines and the baths were deliberately built very small and far apart from each other. Those who managed to get quickly through these two stages of the morning ran to take their place in the longest line of all—the line to the kitchen. Breakfast was modest by any standard: black coffee and a slice of bread with something called jam spread on it. Camp regulations allocated seventy-five minutes for these activities. I must say that there were only a few times when I was able to complete them all. Many times the kitchen window had been shut before I got there to get my miserable breakfast.

At 5:45 A.M. all the prisoners stood at attention in the roll-call yard. Everyone dreaded this morning ceremony. There was always a prisoner who had escaped. There was always an excuse for punishment. For each escaped prisoner the S.S. man on duty would shoot three, four, or five Jews. Whip in hand, he strolled among columns of prisoners, stalking his prey. Then he would point at them with his whip: you, you, you! This order meant "Step out and move to the front!" Then the order was given: "About face!" (*Dreh dich um*), followed by a pistol shot which reverberated in the ominous stillness of the dark dawn and the prisoner fell to the ground. These scenes repeated themselves almost every day.

Daily Routine in the Janowski Camp

On November 18, 1942, my first roll call, the S.S. man Epler was on duty. He was accompanied by askars, Ukrainian policemen, and several civilian respresentatives of German firms who came looking for workers. Only two Jews were shot that morning—one as a punishment for the escape of another prisoner, and another following the complaint of his German employers, who accused him of shirking and lack of productivity. He worked at the ammunition factory. The second item in the roll-call program was "physical exercise"—a sheer farce. One of the minor taskmasters would take over and spit out commands: "Down! Up! Down! Up! Cap off! Cap on!" At the first command all the prisoners fell to the ground and immediately got up. This down-and-up exercise lasted for ten minutes. Then it was time for cap exercises. Those not fast enough doing the up-and-down were beaten mercilessly; the askars and Ukrainian policemen lost no time in seizing the opportunity.

In my column, not far from me, stood a middle-aged Jew. He was thin and scrawny; his face and body were covered with scabs and festering wounds. He was not strong enough to carry out the "up-and-down" orders fast enough. Having fallen down he was unable to get up and when he managed to get up, his legs wobbled. When the "exercise" was over, he raised his hands and cried with a weeping hoarse voice: "Herr Epler, Herr Epler, please have pity on me and shoot me. I can't take it anymore. I don't want to live." Epler and his entourage walked up to him. He understood the Jew's plea. He appraised him briefly and flicked his little finger, telling him to turn his face and show his festering wounds. He gave him another look and decided: "You can still earn your two zloty a day." German firms paid two zloty to the camp management for one day's work of a Jew. This Jew will suffer a little more and live a little longer. Why should he be presented with the gift of mercy killing? Several days later a former student of mine by the name of Zimmerman related to me a similar incident that had taken place in the roll-call yard. It involved the director of the Lvov or-phanage, Czermak, and his twenty-year-old son. They were hauled off to the camp after the August *Aktion* and since then kept together. In early October 1942 a large group of prisoners escaped from the camp. The young Blum, who was the S.S. man on duty that day, picked out, among others, Czermak's son to be executed as a reprisal. Czermak was a man over fifty but he was still very strong. He could not bear the sight of his son being killed and asked the S.S. man to shoot him instead. "He is still young," he said, "and my life has no value." Blum refused. On the contrary, he ordered Czermak senior to stand in the front row to have a good view of the spectacle. I give you another flower (in German and in Yiddish "Blum") in the garland of National Socialism.

All this took place by the light of the projectors and lasted until 6:30 A.M. Then each labor brigade was given its assignment for the day. At about 7:00 A.M. the brigades began leaving for work. We, the new arrivals, were not allowed out yet. We were told to remain in the roll-call yard for registration. Skilled workers such as tailors and mechanics, especially automobile mechanics, were immediately assigned to the DAW brigade. The feeble and sick were incorporated into the cripples brigade. The remainder, me included, were assigned to the brigade of unskilled workers employed at all kinds of dirty jobs. Those assigned to the cripples brigade made a terrifying impression; more dead than alive, they moved with their heads bent, their hopes gone, and their faces indicating that they knew the fate awaiting them in the near future.

We stayed in the camp that day. We were put to work cleaning the barracks, scrubbing floors and walls. We removed the sleeping boards, cleaned them, and aired the straw mattresses, which literally were falling apart in our hands. Rot had eaten into them and they stank to high heaven. During this work we were unable to breathe because of the stench. Ormland commented that he did not remember the barracks having ever been cleaned. Upon finishing our job in late evening, we sneaked into the bathrooms, which were locked for the night, and, having missed the meager supper, dropped on the sleeping boards completely exhausted. Despite the fatigue, I could not fall asleep. In the faint light seeping in through the tiny window above my sleeping board I was able to observe my neighbors. Zimmerman, a former student of mine, was asleep next to me: a nice boy from a very poor family in Zniesienie, an excellent student, intelligent and well read. He earned his living by giving private lessons in mathematics and physics to weak students and even helped his poor parents. Despite his twenty-one years, he looked like a poorly assembled skeleton, a human wreck. After the back-breaking day of work he slept like a stone. A faint glow illuminated his face. I looked at him and his neighbors. A specialist in physiognomy could write volumes about these faces. I do not know what left deeper marks in their faces: thirteen to fifteen months of life in the ghetto or the last four months in the camp which began with the August *Aktion*. I for one think that both these periods equally disfigured the delicate and gentle features, turning them monstrous in appearance. The creased, dirty-yellowish face, the brownish and bluish spots under the eyes, the thin, scrawny body of the young man, did not bear any resemblance to the young, cheerful, and vigorous Zimmerman I had known.

To my left slept Haim Rosenfeld, a seventeen-year-old boy, son of Rabbi Hersh Rosenfeld, the religious judge of the Zniesienie district. His parents, two sisters, and younger brother were sent to Belzec, whereas he stayed behind in the camp. Where have his cheerfulness and alertness gone? I spotted my other former students asleep on the sleeping boards nearby; it was they who found me a place in Barracks no. 5. Here slept Rysiek Weinstock, son of one of the editors of *Chwila* a Jewish newspaper appearing in Polish. Chanales, Zeif, and many others, all seventeen-, eighteen-, twenty-year-olds, were also here. Master of the world, what happened to all these children? They had the faces of wrinkled old men. The barracks sank into a deep, anxious sleep. Now and then a strange snoring could be heard sounding like a cry, or a deep stifled groan; the prisoners dream about the events of the past day.

At dawn the roll call with its usual routine was repeated. Our brigades of simple workers are lined up by the gate, waiting to leave for work. Nearby an orchestra consisting of the well-known Lvov musicians plays: Yakov Mond, Leo Shtricks, Leo Shaff, Yosef Orman, Edward Steinberg. On my first departure for work their playing was an absolute nightmare. It was humiliating and depressing. The sounds of the Radetzky march, brutally and cynically reminded the Jews: You will never enjoy real music in a concert hall; perhaps you are hearing Jewish musicians playing for the last time in your life.

Engelhart of the S.S. brought us to our place of work at a building at Kadecka [Kordecki] Street where Polish officers once lived and a cadet school operated. We were assigned the job of cleaning the houses, painting the rooms, furnishing the apartments, and tending the weed-filled gardens. We were escorted and guarded by two Jewish policemen and two askars. The furniture had to be transported from the Supplies Department of the Judenrat. As the manager of these houses, Engelhart of the S.S. was responsible for reconverting them to living quarters. He assigned me to the group of workers charged with bringing the furniture from the Supplies Department into the apartments. There were four of us in the crew: the old Meir, a sixty-six-year-old, still strong in body, a regular worshipper and member of the board of my synagogue Scheinache; the young Halperin who was always telling me about his father, a Hasidic rabbi living in America; the high school teacher Shapiro, about forty years old, but weak; and I who was then thirty-nine.

Hauling heavy furniture to six-story houses at Kadecka [Kordecki] Street was hardly easy work. The main burden fell on Halperin and me. Now and then Engelhart, whip in hand, would sneak up from behind; if he happened to catch us sitting and resting between floors, he showered us with blows on the head. He also delayed us until late in the evening, so that we usually missed supper and went to bed on empty stomachs. Meir and Shapiro collapsed after the first week. I saw they were burning down like candles. On Thursday, December 4, a rigorous

selection took place. The policemen removed from the columns everyone who looked weak or sick and ordered them to undergo the
notorious running test on the sharp cobblestones called cat heads. Meir
and Shapiro failed the test and did not return. At the gate we received
two young prisoners from the new arrivals. Although the work bene-
fited from this, the pain over the death of two dear Jews robbed me of
my sleep. From my bread pouch I removed the fifty-year calendar, a gift
from old Meir in my first days in the camp. I leafed through it, as a
kaddish of sorts for an old friend. To whom shall I tell the date of his
death? Who will say kaddish for him? For him and for thousands of
other victims? In all likelihood, today, Thursday, December 4, 1942,
Meir and Shapiro were shot.

Suddenly I remembered: Lord, today is the day to light the first
candle of Hanukkah. Friday morning, the twenty-fifth of the month of
Kislev. The first candle of Hanukkah and I forgot. My thoughts started
racing. In my mind I began to compare the Hasmonaean period with
our own tragedy. Then we were victorious. But even today there are
Jews who escape from the ghetto and continue to fight in the Polish
woods, weapon in hand, against the archmurderers of human history.
This thought was like a faint but clear ray of hope in the dark and
gloomy night of 25 Kislev 1942 in the Lvov death camp. I woke up my
neighbor and started searching for a candle like a man possessed. After
a short while I found two candle ends and a match.

"Jews!" I cried out like a madman. "Jews! Today is the day of the
first candle of Hanukkah? Jews? Listen to the blessing over the first
candle of Hanukkah!" The barracks stirred, electrified. Human
shadows rose from their sleeping boards and started crawling toward
my top bunk, toward my candle end. Voices were heard: "What does he
want? Who is he? Who dares to say blessings over the Hanukkah
candles? The askars will kill us in short order."

"Let him say the blessing, let him," said the others. My voice grew
stronger and began to pervade the barracks. I said the blessings with a
strong and confident voice. The prisoners grew quiet, my voice could
be heard in every corner. "We light these candles to commemorate the
miracles and wonders. . . ." I spoke of the miracle of Hanukkah, about
the bright period in our history, when weak and vulnerable we stood up
against the far superior might of the Greeks and yet we were privileged
to witness the miracle of Hanukkah, "for You delivered mighty war-
riors into the hands of the weak, and the many into the hands of the
few." I spoke of steadfastness and hope. It seemed as if my words fell

like a cool, enlivening rain on scorched, arid soil. Barracks no. 5 was all ears, like the enchanted son of the king who has dropped his filthy, lice-infected garments and whose spirit soars aloft. Someone intoned: "Mighty Rock of my salvation . . ." [a Hanukkah hymn]. The singing resounded in the barracks.

Without warning Ormland and a group of Jewish policemen burst into the barracks. "Madmen! You feel like singing, do you!" They dealt blows right and left. They jumped on the sleeping boards, hit prisoners, and flung them onto the floor.

Slowly the barracks returned to normal. Ormland and his gang have won. Truth be told, the singing could have spelled disaster for us.

Christmastime was drawing near. On December 24 we hoped to enjoy a little rest in the camp, but all we got was leaving for work at nine and no roll call. Our crew from Kordecki Street joined a large clean-up brigade working in the city center. We walked down Janowska Street toward Kazimierzowska Street and were approaching the large Polish church of Saint Anna. It was nearly 10:00 A.M. and large crowds of worshippers streamed out of the church, having just finished participating in the Mass celebrating Jesus' birth. The worshippers seemed to be in high spirits, their faces radiated satisfaction. They certainly must have listened to a rousing sermon by the priest who doubtless dwelt on the fact that with the birth of "that man" the good tidings had been fulfilled, as were the words of the prophets about peace, justice, and rectitude, about loving one's neighbor, and that since then the most sublime human ideals have been ruling the world. These ideas are reflected in Polish folk songs celebrating Christmas, the so-called *koledy* [carols]. One of these songs, perhaps the most beautiful one, tells of the glory in heaven and the soft peace which has descended to earth since that time. The refrain of this song is: "*Chwala na wysokosci a na ziemi spokoj*" (Glory on high and peace reigns on earth). But the worshippers leaving the church seemed to have given it a different interpretation. Upon seeing us, the camp prisoners, they burst into a song: "*Chwala na wysokosci, polamali Zydom kosci, a na ziemi spokoj*" (Glory on high, they broke the Jews' bones, and peace reigns on earth). They sang these words to the tune of the carol and it was quite clear that the song was well known in the Polish street. I want to believe that in the crowd that greeted us with this nasty song there were honest people who were grieved by this expression of hatred. I continue to believe in human beings created in the image of God. There must be among them persons who had sheltered Jews and risked their lives in doing so. But unfortunately, they belonged to a negligible minority. The majority believed and acted differently. At the most they did not show any reaction and went past our tragedy with indifference. The two-thousand-year-old theory about Jews as "killers of God" bore its fruit in these stormy times.

About the middle of December I went through a very difficult day which caused me a great deal of pain and grief. On the morning of our departure for work, there were three large trucks waiting at the gate to take us to the old graveyard at Szpitalna Street. At the graveyard two S.S. men were waiting. They ordered us to pull down the tombstones and load them onto the trucks. Wielding axes and shovels we set about this dreadful work of sacrilege. This was perhaps the oldest Jewish cemetery in all eastern Galicia. It was inaugurated in the thirteenth century and closed in 1855. This graveyard was a silent testimony to the vibrant Jewish life in Lvov. Rabbis, heads of yeshivot, great Torah scholars, important Jewish personages lay buried here, as well as Sephardic Torah scholars who had settled in Lvov after their expulsion from Spain in 1492 and who had probably founded the first Torah study institution in Galicia. In the winter of 1941, the Religious Affairs Department of the Judenrat decided to undertake a project of photographing and recording the inscriptions on the tombstones in the graveyard in order to gather materials for future historians. I knew a group of youths who took upon themselves this holy mission, but the photographs and documents must have disappeared together with the Jews who compiled them. And now with my own hands I pulled down these holy stones. It seemed to me that I was tearing a beating heart from the living body of Lvov Jewry, a body that was in its death throes. When the three trucks were full we went back on foot to Kordecki Street, where we unloaded the tombstones and used them to pave the paths in each block of buildings of the former officers' school. We were busy pulling down tombstones and paving paths with them for a whole week. Later other crews were assigned to this work.

On January 1, 1943, we did not work and stayed in the camp; this was the only day of rest I remember from the camp. Most of the barracks dwellers seized the opportunity to have a good sleep before getting a bullet in the head and slept throughout the day. Another group sang folk songs. But everyone was enraptured by a cantor from one of the townships in east Galicia who sang whole chapters of Selikhoth with a beautiful tenor. His interpretation of the prayer "We are the most guilty of all people, our generation is the most shame-covered" left a profound impression on us. I explained to my comrades the topicality of these words. "What have we been punished for? Are we worse than other nations, than previous generations?" Voices of my listeners rose in protest: "Why? How is it possible? Where is the justice of the Maker of the world?" I tried to expound the meaning of the profound concept of "veiled countenance"; in certain periods of our history Providence veils its face and its life-giving, health-giving, joy-giving, and hope-giving rays bounce off the iron wall and fail to reach us. My explanations and words of comfort rang hollow in their ears and were met with disbelief. But how could they react in any other way? I faced people who had lost hope, people chastened by bitter experience, despairing people who had lost everything—father and mother, wife and children, people whose only possession was their own naked life which was bound to be taken away from them, if not today then tomorrow. How could they be comforted? For want of anything better they returned to the sorrowful tune of "we are the most guilty of all people." It struck me then that Moses, our teacher, was in a similar situation when in the Egyptian forced labor camp he tried to comfort his people with the promise of a bright future awaiting them. But as we are told in the book of Exodus (6:9): "But they hearkened not unto Moses for anguish of spirit and for cruel bondage." If Moses himself could not find the words to instill hope in the hearts of the inmates of the forced labor camp in Egypt, who was I to find them?

With the completion of work at Kordecki Street our crew was disbanded and its members dispersed among other crews. I was transferred to the sanitation brigade which was regarded as a comparatively good assignment. There were several hundred workers in the brigade and a single individual would not stand out. But the most important thing was that we worked at garbage collection in various parts of the city, which enabled us to maintain contact with the external world. Despite the fact that we were well guarded, we managed to receive bulletins from the Polish and Jewish underground from time to time. News from the war fronts lifted our spirits and provided some hope.

On January 5, 1943, we left for work as usual. In the city center the brigade split into different groups assigned to different parts of town. My group was sent to Zielona Street to collect garbage from the courtyards. A Pole approached and asked whether I knew what was happening in the ghetto. It turned out that a terrible *Aktion* was underway there. Upon our return to the camp in the evening we found a scene of confusion. Large crowds of ghetto residents were milling about, awaiting their fate. Delivering fierce blows with rifle butts, the policemen loaded people onto large trucks which then drove to the Kleparow railway station. From there trains of sealed cars bound with barbed wire left for Belzec. Only a few of the ghetto residents, the young, were left in the camp. The *Aktion* raged for three days, from January 5 to 7, 1943. This January *Aktion* swallowed up some fifteen thousand Jews. Immediately afterward the ghetto area was reduced, the Judenrat was disbanded and all its staff incarcerated in the camp or shot. Then the last chairman of the Judenrat, Dr. Ebersohn, was shot together with members of his board, Higger, Dr. Kimmelman and Dr. Buber. Two other members of the board, Dr. Shretzer [Szerer] and Dr. Leib Landau, succeeded in fleeing and hiding in the Aryan section. Later someone informed on them; they were caught, thrown into the Jewish prison at Zamenhof Street and then shot.

The Germans turned the reduced ghetto into a Jewish camp—*Judenlager,* "Julag" for short. They introduced strict military discipline under the command of a German commandant, Grzymek, and his staff: Mansfeld, Siler, and Heinisch. Grzymek was a blood-thirsty beast, plain and simple. Every day he shot dozens of Jews on the pretext of keeping the Julag clean. Grzymek appointed Feil as the *Ober-Jude* of the Julag, but the man had no influence whatsoever on living conditions there.

At that time I didn't feel well. I kept on working, hoping that the pain would pass. In the meantime my temperature rose and I could barely lift my feet. Earlier I had struck up a friendship with one of the several physicians in our brigade, Dr. Szor, from the town of Rzeszow. In the evening he examined me, took my temperature, and determined that I had contracted typhus. I had two options: to report my illness to the camp authorities and be hospitalized or to ignore it and carry on working. Entering the camp hospital meant certain death.

The hospital was located in a barracks declared unfit for housing prisoners. There was no sanitary equipment whatsoever and apparently no medicines or medical instruments. It was winter and the barracks were not heated. Its director, Dr. Maksymilian Kurcrok, was a warm-hearted Jew but he too was a camp prisoner; he had no means to treat his patients except with comforting words. The S.S. men Brombauer and Bormann were the rulers of the hospital. Now and then they would come inside, remove the sickest or the unconscious and shoot them. Only a handful came out of there alive and intact.

It came as no surprise that under these conditions sick inmates avoided being hospitalized, tried to hold out, and kept working. Fellow prisoners showed great devotion in caring for their sick comrades. The most dangerous moment was after the roll call, at the checkpoint at the main gate. Once the S.S. man on duty spotted a sick prisoner, he would immediately remove him from the column and place him in between the double row of barbed wire fence, thus passing the death sentence on him. Comrades of sick prisoners, the entire work crew, went to great lengths to shield them from the eyes of the S.S. man at the checkpoint. I chose to work and all the members of my crew helped me, particularly my two guardian angels, Dr. Szor from Rzeszow and my friend Gross. The latter was a sportsman, a professional boxer well known in Lvov. In mid-January 1943 our crew worked at the Kleparow railway station; we unloaded coal from the cars and loaded it onto large trucks. At the first attempt the shovel slipped from my hands. More than once I received a beating, but did not give up and carried on even when my temperature went up to 40° Celsius. Only in the evening, when lying on my sleeping board, did I allow myself to be sick. To this day I do not understand how I managed to pull through.

I can think of no other explanation than that Providence watched over me. In the most difficult moments at the Kleparow railway station, in between the coal cars, I gritted my teeth and kept muttering: "Even when the blade of a sharp sword, . . ." etc. Using various ploys Dr. Szor would acquire caffeine and sometimes other medicines for me. At the checkpoint he and the boxer Gross locked hands with me and passed me through. In this way I got through my most difficult period in the camp, the days of my illness. Somehow I made it. There were hundreds of typhus victims like me in the camp. They went through indescribable agonies, almost went out of their minds, but many survived.

In early February I was transferred to the VIB (*Vereinigte Industrie Betriebe*) brigade. This was the easiest assignment; some members of the brigade even stayed in the factory for the night shift.

VIB produced for the Wehrmacht. Our factory was located at Zamarstynowska Street and manufactured cutlery for the German military at the front. Skilled workers made aluminum casts of spoons, forks, knives, and teaspoons, whereas we polished them, first on a machine and then manually. Our supervisor was a Polish *Volksdeutsche* by the name of Schtentzel. Always irritated and unsatisfied, he walked among the worktables and kept demanding higher daily output. But all in all I was very pleased to be working in the VIB brigade since it gave me access to Jews from the Julag.

Now and then crews of VIB workers were furnished with a special official pass and dispatched to the raw material warehouse located in a side alley off Zamarstynowska Street. For a period, this pass enabled me to gain a certain freedom of movement and enter houses in the Julag. The *Ober-Jude* Haim Feil revealed to me that there were some fifteen thousand Jews in the Julag: about twelve thousand skilled workers employed by German firms and three thousand elderly, parents, women, and children. Grzymek regarded workers as the only legal residents of the Julag. Others resided there illegally and their lives were in danger. Hunted down by Grzymek and his underlings, their number decreased with each passing day. Every day, however, new Jews entered the Julag; they had escaped from the *Aktionen* in the environs of Lvov and from small towns in eastern Galicia. Among the new arrivals were also jumpers from the trains bound for Belzec. They would sneak into the ghetto at night, stripped of everything, looking like ghosts. The illegal residents of the Julag, themselves being hunted, opened their doors and hearts to them.

Returning from work one day in the middle of February 1943, I came across a group of jumpers on Janowska Street. It was freezing cold and they were practically naked. When they had been loaded onto a train bound for Belzec at the Kleparow railway station, the Germans had taken away their clothing to prevent escapes. This failed to deter them and they jumped off the train. Right away we took off all our outer garments, clothed them, and showed them the way to the Julag. Not a living soul could be seen on the street. Christian residents of Lvov refrained from staying outdoors in the evening.

The *Ober-Jude* Feil told me that the only institution recognized by Grzymek was the Burials Department—the *Hevra-Kadisha*. Every day people died and every day people were shot. The dead were being buried at the Janowska Street graveyard. A number of community officials working for the Burials Department, located in a side alley called Zamarsztynow, performed this work. From Feil I learned that there were a number of rabbis among them and I made up my mind to find them. Pass in hand, I set about looking for the Zamarsztynow alley and shortly thereafter found the small building of the *Hevra-Kadisha*. The one-story building was surrounded by a tall fence. Along the fence stood a large, long barracks. Management of the graveyard was done from the ground floor, whereas the families lived on the second floor. Bodies covered with canvas sheets lay on the ground inside the barracks.

Bodies were carted off to the graveyard every day, sometimes even several times a day, especially after an *Aktion,* or when mortality was higher than usual. The killed were buried in their clothes as prescribed by law. Bodies of the "regular" dead were rarely subjected to the ritual of purification—there was not enough manpower for the job. Three rabbis, together with their families, worked for the Burials Department: Rabbi Zeltenreich from Wadowice, Rabbi Abraham Frenkel (son-in-law of the rabbi from Wadowice, if I remember correctly), and Rabbi Hirshhorn from Biala-Podolska. By that time not one of the Lvov rabbis was still alive; all either had perished in the *Aktion* or had died of typhus. My friend, Rabbi Kalman Chameides, the rabbi of Katowice, died of typhus during the November *Aktion.*

People in the Camp

Throughout the entire period of my incarceration in the Janowski camp I never met a rabbi. I believe this is due to the fact that in various *Aktionen* in cities and small towns, the Germans murdered rabbis and religious judges first. They didn't even bother taking them away but murdered them on the spot in front of their congregations. My fellow camp inmates told me about murders of their towns' rabbis. I was told of several incidents in which the local rabbi inveighed against his murderers and comforted his congregation by emphasizing the great significance of Sanctification of the Name in the history of our people. Only in a few cases did the murderers allow a rabbi to finish his oratory; they usually cut it short with a bullet. The shooting was done by an S.S. man. Rabbis from the Burials Department told me similar stories. Rabbi Zeltenreich showed me a list of rabbis from Galicia who had died for the Sanctification of the Name.

Our conversation on this subject was interrupted by a warning of an impending visit of Grzymek. His sudden visits always aroused fear and panic. Sure enough, the whole place was transformed. Women and other visitors who had come here to arrange burials fled in panic, looking for a place to hide. Children ran outside screaming and disappeared inside the large barracks. As a camp inmate holding a special pass I was protected. It turned out that this time the ruler of the Julag came demanding information about the activities of the Burials Department: statistics on the dead, the number of caretakers, and so on. After he left, taking with him the statistical material, everyone came back to life and returned to his place. Children also returned and asked us amidst bursts of laughter: "Do you know where we hid? Among the dead, under the canvas sheets." The children were no more than eight, ten, twelve years old. If this is not a nightmare, what is?

On a cold and gloomy morning in early March 1943, we went through one of the most trying experiences in the camp. At roll-call time we noticed that a small stage of sorts with a few stairs leading up to it stood next to the main gate. All this was surrounded with barbed wire. The stage stood on one side of the gate and the orchestra on the other side. That day we were delayed and did not leave for work right away after roll call. The camp commandant, *Obersturmfuehrer* Willhaus himself, put in an appearance. As he stepped to the front of the stage, we were struck with mortal fear. Who knew what "news" lay in store for us today? Willhaus began speaking slowly and deliberately, casting friendly glances toward the colums of workers. "True," he said, "we demand work of you, serious work, but we also take care of you and we are going to give you some entertainment. Beginning today we will treat you to an interesting spectacle while you leave for work. As you can see we take good care of you and we even brought a special orchestra. Beginning today you'll be able to enjoy yourselves and see special dancers in action who will dance original Jewish dances for you." At that point Willhaus gave a sign to the askars and from a side alley two Jews emerged. They were escorted, or, to be more exact, driven, by an S.S. man who with his whip forced them to mount the stage. Then he stood on the lowest step, cracked his whip, and shouted: *"Sing Jude sing, tanz Jude tanz"* (Sing Jew, sing, dance, Jew, dance). One of the dancers was a man over sixty, of medium height, with a beard and sidelocks, the noble face of a scholar, blue deep eyes reflecting the depth of Jewish sorrow and suffering. He wore a torn silk caftan with shreds hanging from every side. His wide-brimmed hat was creased and soiled; in his hand he held a broken red umbrella. The second Jew was a tall, middle-aged man with a thick, black, matted beard. The sleeve of his jacket was missing, his trousers were all tatters, and his skin could be seen through numerous holes in his garment. He wore a skullcap; a large red kerchief, which he waved like a flag, had been thrust into his hand. The two moved about the small stage, dancing and singing in a weeping voice: "Oh, Lord, please save us."

The spectacle took place every day and lasted for an hour until all the workers had left the gate. Whenever the two victims slackened the pace of their dance or their voices weakened, the whip of the S.S. man went to work right away: "Sing Jew, dance Jew!"

Later I learned that the Jew with a red umbrella was Rabbi Feibisch of Jaworow and both Jews were natives of the same small town in eastern Galicia. In the first days of March 1943, a terrible *Aktion* was raging in Jaworow. These two were brought to the Janowski camp together with other victims from that locality. This explains the name Feibisch Jaworower (Feibisch from Jaworow)—I never learned his real name. Both were selected in one of the *Aktionen* and brought here to "cheer up" the prisoners. The show made a dreadful impression on us. The nation of "poets and thinkers" did not content itself with tormenting Jews physically, with starving and oppressing them to the point where every day they looked death in the eyes, but also added humiliations, trampling underfoot and spitting on Jewish dignity and human values.

About two weeks after his first "appearance," I met Rabbi Feibisch in the barracks near the kitchen. I shook his hand with a warm *Shalem aleykhem* greeting. We were silent. All the questions such as "Where does the Jew come from? seemed trifling and banal to me. There was no point in either my questions or words of comfort. I stood face to face with a man personifying the fate of the people of Israel at this time and all I felt was utter helplessness. In fact, I was almost embarrassed. I simply could not open my mouth. It was Rabbi Feibisch who spoke: "How shall we sing the Lord's song in a strange land?" He understood my hesitation and my embarrassment and went straight to the heart of the matter. This verse of Psalms (87:4) sent me back to the time of the destruction of the First Temple in 587 BCE, when the conquerors and destroyers of the temple demanded of the Levites: "Sing us one of the songs of Zion" and the Levites replied: "How shall we sing the Lord's song in a strange land?" In a soft voice and with a bowed head, as if talking to himself, he related his story to me. All members of his family had been shot. He alone was left alive and brought here. Rabbi Feibisch fell silent for a moment and continued: "The Midrash says that when the Levites were called to play and sing, they bit their fingers and replied: 'How shall we sing?'"

In fact, in his memoirs of the return from Babylon to Israel, Ezra the Scribe relates that in preparation for rebuilding the Temple he could not find any Levites: "And I viewed the People and the priests and found there none of the sons of Levi" (Ezra 8:15). Rashi interprets this verse (Babylonian Talmud, tractate Kiddushin 69:b) as follows: "Why could he not find qualified and suitable Levites for officiating in the Temple service? Because when Nebuchadnezzar told them 'sing us one of the songs of Zion,' they held themselves in check, bit their thumbs off and said: 'How shall we sing the Lord's song in a strange land?' Now the verse does not say 'we shall not sing' but 'how shall we sing,' meaning 'we cannot pluck the harp strings.' These were the Levites who came with Ezra from Babylon, but qualified Levites did not arrive." This is how Rashi makes a case for his commentary with the Midrash Yalkuth Shimoni, Psalm 84. I said to myself: Blessed are the Levites who "held themselves in check," whereas he, Rabbi Feibisch in the accursed Janowski camp, couldn't he do the same despite the whip of the S.S. murderer? Not saying a word I stood by his side for a long time and heard him crying. His weeping and groans haunt me to this very day.

One day in the middle of March, the stage disappeared and we saw the dancing Jews no more. The Germans must have become bored with this devilish and cruel pastime and simply liquidated the two Jews.

In the meantime I was transferred to another VIB work crew. I believe that my transfer was effected by Rysiek Oskar who was the office head, responsible for work registration, and could thus exercise some influence on work assignments. VIB enjoyed a good reputation among the camp prisoners. Human quality there was higher and more camaraderie prevailed among the workers, who included many intellectuals and even religious scholars. Nighttime conversations among the occupants of the sleeping boards often resembled the symposia from the good old days before the war. Jewish camp policemen tended to be more lenient here, turned a blind eye to certain things, and did not disrupt morning, evening, or Sabbath prayers. There were a number of writers among us: Karol Drezner, Yerahmiel Green, Daniel Oker, David Fraenkel, and other Jewish literary figures and intellectuals from various cities and small towns whose names I do not recall. Occasionally they read us their poems and essays. We often debated philosophical questions that did not bear at all on our gruesome reality. On the contrary, we sought to escape from it, to enjoy to the full the few weeks of relative calm that had befallen us in the camp. Now and then we read and interpreted chapters of the Bible. Particularly vivid responses were aroused by chapter 26 of the book of Leviticus ("If you walk in my statutes . . .") and chapter 28 of the book Deuteronomy—the chastisement.

I read the tragic chapters of the prophecy of Jeremiah. A stormy controversy erupted over the words in chapter 12: "Righteous art Thou, O Lord, when I plead with Thee: yet let me talk with Thee of

Thy judgments. Wherefore doth the way of the wicked prosper? Wherefore are they all happy that deal very treacherously?" The age-old query "Why do the righteous suffer and the evildoers prosper?" acquired utmost urgency. The same question again and again: "Why? Where is God's righteous man?" The suffering Job asked: "Wherefore do the wicked live, become old, yea, are mighty in power?" (Job 21:7). The same Job also tried to answer the grave question in chapter 28. Several times he said: "Whence then cometh wisdom? And where is the place of understanding? Seeing it is hid from the eyes of all living and kept close from the fowls of the air" (Job 28:20–21). And in fact are we capable of grasping the ways and plans of Providence with our limited human concepts of justice and righteousness? "Man knoweth not the price thereof . . . seeing it is hid from the eyes of all living."

At VIB I had a dear friend, David Shapiro, a native of a remote village in the Carpathian mountains. He was a self-taught scholar, a well-read man, an ardent Czurtkow Hasid, and, above all, a noble and dear soul. One day he returned from work carrying a rare and dangerous find. He had found the burned remains of the talmudic tractate Ketuboth. Only the two last chapters were intact. That night we conducted a Talmud study session and became absorbed in a very interesting tale. "Rabanan taught: a person should always live in the land of Israel, even in a city predominantly pagan, and must not live outside the land of Israel even in a city inhabited mostly by Jews. For he who lives in the land of Israel, it is as if he has God, whereas he who lives outside the land of Israel, it is as if he does not have God" (Ketuboth 60:b). It might be worth remembering that this fragment of Talmud and a small Bible in my possession exposed its owner to mortal danger.

The VIB brigade had yet another advantage: one could be assigned to a night shift. When working on aluminum casting of cutlery, we stayed for night shift two or three times a week. Spending the night outside the camp was like winning a lottery prize.

This idyll did not last forever. On March 16, 1943, a prisoner at the S.S. Lovov camp at Czwarty [?] Listopada Street shot an S.S. man to death. Although I do not know the details of this act of revenge by a Jewish prisoner, I witnessed its outcome with my own eyes. The surviving remnant of Lvov Jews paid dearly for this aberrant act of revenge. Twelve Jewish policemen were hanged on Lokietek Street. In the Julag, Grzymek unleashed a terrible *Aktion,* in the course of which over one thousand Jews were shot in the "sands." In our camp Willhaus and his underlings wiped out an entire brigade. Later we were told that on that day more than two hundred camp prisoners were killed. Life in the camp became unbearable. We felt we were facing a new disaster. A barbaric exercise nicknamed "the vitamin race," which had not been staged recently, was now resumed in the evening after work. It went like this: late in the evening, after a regular day of backbreaking work, all the prisoners were taken out of the camp to the road leading to the Kleparow railway station. S.S. men, askars, and Jewish camp police-men lined up on both sides of the road. The prisoners were given the order: *Laufschritt!*—run! Brigade after brigade, five prisoners in a row, started running to the railway station. Upon arrival each grabbed a board, a load of planks or bricks and ran back quickly to the con-struction yard in the camp. The road was lit seven days a week. Anyone breaking ranks or falling behind was fiercely beaten. The shouts, screams, and shooting of the taskmasters terrorized the prisoners. Each such vitamin race resulted in a number of dead prisoners. The name derived from the vitamins we hauled on our backs: Vitamin B (in Polish *belki*—beams), vitamin C (in Polish *cegly*—bricks), and vitamin D (in Polish *deski*—planks).

In one of the vitamin races I came across Pinye Weber, a friend from childhood days in heder in our native town of Grzymalow. Pinye was forty, healthy, strong, and tall, a man of the people, of penetrating intelligence, a well-read, self-taught person. His mother received the nickname "sitting Minka" because all her life she sat in the marketplace of Hrimalow selling vegetables and fruit. At the age of eighteen she married a young foreigner who had come to our town from Latin America but who left immediately after the wedding without leaving a trace. Minka remained an *agunah* (a wife whose husband has disap-peared without divorcing her) until the Germans killed her. Her son Pinye arrived in the Janowski camp in January 1943. All his life he had been tormented by his mother's tragedy and kept writing letters to the four corners of the earth, seeking to locate this "gem," his father, but he never found him.

Once, toward the end of yet another "vitamin race," I saw Pinye lying like a corpse near the camp gate. He was skin and bones, bleeding, and exhausted after the savage treatment he had just undergone. With the help of other prisoners I brought him back to his barracks, laid him on the sleeping board, and gave him something to eat to bring him back to life. Having regained some of his strength, he spoke and told me his story.

His brigade worked outside. He was strong and enduring, took good care of himself, and felt well. One day, along the barbed-wire fence of women's camp, he recognized his wife. He had left her behind in Grzymalow with a three-year-old child. She told him that during one of the *Aktionen* she had been taken to Tarnopol together with the child and there put on a train bound for Belzec. At night men broke the window and started jumping off the speeding train. She followed suit, but lost her way in the forest, was caught and brought back to the women's camp. And what happened to the child? asked Pinye. She answered something but Pinye made out only a few words: the child remained in the train. At that point something snapped within this strong man. His faith in humanity and his inner composure left him. There was no point in carrying on living, in struggling to survive. If a mother could leave her child on a train bound for Belzec in order to save her own life, life was not worth living. His own mother wouldn't have done such a thing. Pinye made up his mind to desist from further struggling for life which had no meaning. He no longer attended to his work, his nutrition; he was beaten and kept silent. His supervisor saw there was no use for the man and kicked him out of the brigade. The camp management had no pity and was not interested in psychological subtleties or the agonies of the soul. Pinye was transferred to the cripples brigade and waited for death to save him.

This is how I found him that evening after the vitamin race at the camp gate. I tried to comfort him, to instill some faith and hope into his tormented soul. Our history is not unfamiliar with such disasters, I said. Not for nothing is it written in Lamentations: "Even the sea monsters draw out the breast, they give suck to their young ones; the daughter of my people has become cruel, like the ostriches in the wilderness." Yet despite moral depravity, I went on to say, our people rose to greatness, rebuilt their state, and created cultural treasures. One must not give way to despair, and so on. But it was clear to me that my words rang hollow in his ears and his gaze remained fixed on a distant point not in this world.

At the end of March I was surprised to receive a written note from my wife, brought to me by one of our brigade members. At that time she was well hidden in the Studite convent and knew of my incarceration in the Janowski camp. Terrible rumors about the camp prompted her to search for a hiding place for me. Risking her life she waited for several days near the camp gate until she managed to slip a note to one of the prisoners. She wrote that she succeeded in securing for me "a good place at the mother's, where they wait for you." This meant that the prioress (mother of the convent) was willing to hide me. In those days it was relatively easy to escape from the VIB brigade but this could have cost the lives of several fellow prisoners. I struggled with my conscience all night and decided to stay in the camp.

The month of March with its troubles and torments passed and April came with its warm winds heralding the spring. The spring winds brought with them other, ominous tidings—rumors about the terrible extermination *Aktionen,* the final liquidation of the Lvov ghetto, the Julag. Despite these rumors, however, we did not forget it was the month of Nissan and Passover was drawing near. But where could we obtain matzoth and what could we do to refrain from eating leavened bread? I decided to take advantage of the liberal atmosphere in the VIB brigade and the good will of my comrades and set up a meeting with the surviving rabbis in the Julag. One evening, when I was working on the night shift, the following rabbis gathered in the side yard of our factory: Rabbi Zeltenreich and Rabbi Frenkel of Wadowice, Rabbi Halberstamm, the rabbi of Zaklikow (son-in-law of the famous rabbi from Trzebynia, Brish Weidenfeld), Rabbi Twerski of the famous Twerski family, and a few other observant Jews who wished nothing more than to acquire Passover matzoth. I also invited the head of the Julag, or, as the Germans called him, the *Ober-Jude.* He didn't have much influence in the ghetto, but he was Grzymek's servant. He promised that news of this gathering would not leak outside and that he would provide us with flour. We would be able to bake matzoth for the ghetto residents and also a few for the camp prisoners. The man stood by his word.

On April 10 we received two sacks of flour from Feil and got down to work. In a partly destroyed house on Lokietek Street we prepared an oven and baked matzoth as prescribed by law. The organizer and prime mover in this undertaking was Rabbi Twerski; the rest of us served as his assistants. The whole venture was kept secret and only some twenty people knew of its existence. Rabbi Twerski, together with the other rabbis, undertook to distribute the matzoth among the ghetto residents, whereas I was in charge of the same in the VIB brigade. On April 19, I made a Seder in our factory in the middle of the night shift. Fellow prisoners kept a close watch to prevent anyone from taking notice. The Polish manager of the factory, Sewirski, was privy to our secret and helped us with everything. One brought a white tablecloth which we spread on the large worktable. A few bottles of raisin wine and candlesticks with burning candles appeared on the table, as well as a Seder bowl and bitter herbs. There were not enough matzoth. Almost all the prisoners of our brigade demanded matzoth and refused to eat bread during Passover. Before the Seder we said the evening prayers. We said Hallel (Psalms 113–118 recited on festivals) and everyone fell silent. The cantor prayed in a whisper so that nothing, God forbid, could be heard outside. We sat at the Seder as mourners, choking with tears. Now and then somebody wept. I cannot find proper words to describe this Passover Seder on April 19, 1943.

Late at night without a word we dispersed, each to his workplace. Everyone was absorbed by his own thoughts, memories of his home, the Seder night with his family.

On April 22 someone brought news that moved us deeply; one could even say it had an electrifying impact. A clandestine Polish radio station broadcast a report about an uprising in the Warsaw ghetto. The uprising broke out on the eve of Passover, April 19, and the Jews of Warsaw were fighting against the superior forces of the German enemy. We did not cherish any illusions about the outcome of this uneven battle, but we knew that the rebels were saving the Jewish honor trampled by the coarse boots of Hitler's soldiers.

The month of April was charged with tension. Fantastic rumors kept springing up about the fate awaiting the Julag and the Janowski camp. No one knew what each day would bring. One thing was absolutely clear—we were facing a terrible *Aktion*. What we didn't know was whether it would be unleashed against the Julag or the Janowski camp. Unfortunately, the German plan included both.

3 ❧ AMONG STRANGERS

Hiding in Metropolitan Sheptytskyi's Residence

On May 23, 1943, I worked the night shift. Usually workers from the camp reported for duty in the morning. That morning when workers did not come, we realized something was wrong. Several hours later we learned that the camp was under siege and horrific spectacles were taking place there. The Germans were in the process of liquidating six or seven thousand Jews in the camp, to prepare space for healthy Jews from the ghetto due to arrive several days later after its liquidation.

After an hour or so the VIB workshop manager received instructions over the telephone to send all night-shift workers back to the camp. We knew what this meant. Everyone decided to try to save himself in any way he could. No attempt was made to defend ourselves or to organize an escape.

I remained hidden in the cellar throughout the day. When darkness fell, between seven and eight in the evening, I decided to set out for the metropolitan and ask for shelter.

I tore off the yellow camp badge, took off my soiled clothes, and put on trousers and a jacket someone had given me earlier. Then silently I climbed over the fence, left the factory compound, and walked confidently down the city streets as if I weren't a Jew at all and no one would recognize me. I was headed toward Jura Square.

Jura Square was near the Jesuit garden which had to be crossed in order to arrive at the gate of the metropolitan's palace. This, however, necessitated passing through Gestapo guards patrolling around the square. They went back and forth. Having spotted them from a distance I slowed down and when they went past I slipped by in the darkness (streets were unlit) and started crawling up the slope of the mountain until I reached the gate. I pulled the handle of the bell and waited for the gate to open. I must have waited no more than three or four minutes but they seemed like an eternity. I flattened myself against the gate but was able to hear the heavy steps of the Gestapo men walking back and forth. They did not notice me.

At last the window in the gate opened and the monk asked me: "Who are you? What do you want? " (he spoke in Ukrainian).

I replied: "I am Rabbi Kahane. Please go and tell Metropolitan Sheptytskyi that I want to see him."

"Now, at night? This is dangerous."

He closed the window and let me wait outside. Another five, perhaps ten minutes passed which again seemed an eternity. My heart was beating like mad and I heard the heavy steps of the Gestapo men walking back and forth.

All of a sudden the gate was opened and the monk pulled me inside. I was close to fainting. He closed the gate behind me and led me to the metropolitan's palace.

I was soiled and infested with lice. My clothes were in tatters. The jacket and trousers someone had given me in the ghetto seemed to me like decent garments but from the look in the monk's eyes I knew they were horrid. He brought me to the cellar where I washed and cleaned myself, and he gave me fresh underwear and clothing. He immediately tossed my soiled and lice-infested garments into the burning oven. Just before 11:00 P.M. I completed my ablutions.

The metropolitan was waiting for me despite the late hour and greeted me with great kindness. His good, wise eyes did not change. You will stay here, they seemed to say, you will be taken care of.

"Tell me please," began metropolitan, "what you have been going through since we met last summer. You are surely aware that during your stay in the camp we received many children. I can tell you the names of priests who took them under their care. The children are in good hands and benefit from good education. And now I am ready to help you too."

I told him about the camp, about the atrocities and brutal treatment, about the killings, about roll calls. I also told him about the day in which six to seven thousand Jews were put to death and about the impending liquidation of the ghetto. As I related the story of the ghetto and the camp and the dreadful living conditions of the Jews there, I saw tears rolling down his cheeks. Our conversation lasted for three-quarters of an hour.

At the end of our meeting he delivered me to the care of his brother, Abbot Kliment Sheptytskyi, whom he summoned to his room at the end of our conversation. The abbot led me to the large library room of the Jura Mountain palace. For the time being this was to be my residence.

The room contained the private library of the metropolitan, which probably comprised over one thousand volumes. In one of the corners a hiding place was prepared for me. It was surrounded with books on all sides and a person entering the library could not notice that someone was hidden behind the books. I was not given a bed, but a lounge chair on which I could sleep or rest. For the time being I remained there.

First, a few words about the cathedral named after Saint George which is linked with Archbishop Sheptytskyi's palace. This is the Church of Saint George (*katedra Sw. Jura*) where Metropolitan Sheptytskyi officiates. The building emanates great splendor; it was built in the rococo style by the architect Bernard Merderer who lived in Lvov in the mid-eighteenth century and left a legacy of many buildings in the city.

Who is the metropolitan, the man who accorded me his protection? Who is this man who treated Jews with such great kindness, who pitied them so much, and who accepted so many Jewish children in his monastery?

His lineage goes back to the thirteenth century. In the remote past the Sheptytskyis were a family of *boyars* (Russian noblemen), mentioned in the chronicle of the life and deeds of Prince Lev, the founder of Lvov. A *boyar* by the name of Sheptytskyi, the first recorded ancestor of our metropolitan, was in the circle of Prince Lev. The metropolitan once told me: "I come from an ancient stock, like the stock of the Habsburgs." The clan of Sheptytskyis resided in its family estate Przylbicze near Jaworow. Many of the present metropolitan's ancestors served as archbishops of the Ukrainian population even before the union with the Vatican. One of them was the metropolitan of Lvov and Halicz, whose full title was Metropolitan Halicki.

Over generations his family became assimilated into Polish culture as were many aristocratic Ukrainian families in eastern Galicia. The present metropolitan was born into the family of Count Sheptytskyi, which had become thoroughly Polonized. He was born on July 29, 1865, on the family estate Przylbicze near Jaworow. His mother, Zofia, was the daughter of Count Aleksander Fredro, a renowned Polish poet and playwright, whereas his father was a Polish assimilationist, although proud of his aristocratic Ukrainian lineage. His parents' home was deeply religious and young Roman (his first name) was brought up in the spirit of religion by both his father and his mother.

From his early youth Roman was inclined toward the priesthood and was reported to have said often that he wanted to become a priest. In those days the Ukrainian church was part of the Uniate Christianity (the name derives from the union of the Ukrainian Church and the Vatican). In liturgy it was Eastern Orthodox.

His inclination to the priesthood was combined with sympathy toward the Ukrainian national movement. He sought to return to his national origins, to the Ukrainian people. His father, Count Iohan Sheptytskyi, and his mother, Zofia née Fredro, opposed both his ordination as a priest and his conversion to Ukrainian nationalism and renunciation of the Polonized cultural environment. They worked hard to dissuade him when Roman was still a student at a gymnasium. Upon graduation he was sent to Germany to study law and he graduated with honors and a Doctor of Law degree.

Roman's views and sympathies were fully shared by his brother Kazimierz, the future Abbot Kliment Sheptytskyi. The third brother, Stanislaw, refused to become a Ukrainian and remained a Pole. Later he became a general in the Polish army and remained a Pole until his death.

After taking his law degree, Roman Sheptytskyi decided to travel to Italy in order to pay a visit to the pope, Leo XIII, to seek his advice on his future. During his visit to the pope in 1886, Roman decided to abandon the Roman Catholic church and join the Uniate Catholic church. He also made up his mind to enter a theological seminary to study toward a degree in theology and to become a priest.

He spoke with the pope about the situation of the Uniate church in eastern Galicia and made him quite an audacious proposal: he announced his plans to become head of the Uniate Catholic church in the Ukraine and to bring it into the fold of the Vatican. The pope gave his blessing to the project and promised to give it his support.

Upon his return home, Roman announced to his parents his plan to join a monastery, to study theology, and to become a priest. His parents were vehemently opposed to the plan, but after prolonged arguments they yielded and gave their consent.

He joined the Basilian Order, guided by the idea that had become the signpost of his life: to bring about the unification of the Ukrainian Eastern Orthodox church with the Uniate church.

With three doctorates to his name—in philology, theology, and law—he began serving as a priest and his career advanced rapidly. His first high-ranking post was the archbishopric of Stanislawow and afterward he was appointed the metropolitan of Lvov.

Roman Sheptytskyi of yesterday, and Andrei Sheptytskyi of today, the metropolitan of the Uniate Catholic church, a scion of an ancient *boyar* family, whose ancestors had sat on the archbishop's throne in Lvov, was received enthusiastically by the Ukrainian masses and the whole population of the Ukraine, including Jews who knew that the man was destined to play a crucial role in the life of the Ukrainian people in eastern Galicia and the Uniate Catholic Church.

One of his first acts was the founding of the Studite Order in 1906. Studites were a society of monks devoted exclusively to the worship of God and to helping people wherever they were—at home and at work. They lived in communal monasteries, but most of them worked outside wherever they could. Members of the order included those in lay professions, workers, peasants, and others who sought to renounce secular life and devote themselves to helping others. All the waking hours of the Studite monk were devoted to work and prayer.

At the time of the founding of the monastery, the metropolitan's brother, Count Kazimierz Sheptytskyi, was a forty-year-old lawyer of great renown and a member of the Parliament in Vienna. Andrei persuaded him to abandon his secular profession, enter a seminary, become ordained as a priest, and assume the responsibilities of head (abbot) of the Studite Order. Kazimierz changed his name to Kliment and became head of all the Studite monasteries, which in the future were to play an important role in rescuing Jews.

Monasteries which engaged in saving Jews, particularly in sheltering Jewish children, included the one at Piotr Skarga Street in Lvov. It was known for its famous library of Byzantine studies ("Studyon"), containing thousands of volumes. Others were the Kuszewicz monastery near Lvov; "Unif" near Przemyslane, the central Studite monastery; and the Pidlute Lyzki monastery. Convents included Liczakow located at Obucz alley—its Abbess Iosefa (last name Witter) was head of all Studite convents; those in Jekatorov, attached to "Unif"; and Brzuchowice, with its children's home. Studite convents also managed children's houses outside of the convent.

In Lvov, Metropolitan Andrei plunged vigorously into cultural activities among his people to whose heritage he had returned from the bosom of his Polonized family. He fought relentlessly against the policies of Polonization pursued by Ukrainian Poles and later by the Polish government. He fought discrimination against Ukrainians, worked toward raising their cultural and moral standards, and displayed a friendly attitude toward the Jews.

In his archives I found letters addressed to representatives of the Lvov Jewish community. He almost never missed an opportunity to extend material assistance to poor Jews before Passover to help them buy matzoth. He gave Passover alms. Along with the check he always enclosed a note with words of friendship toward Jews. One letter was written by him personally in biblical high-flown Hebrew. A well-known antiquarian and bookseller in Lvov, Naftali Siegel, was his Hebrew teacher.

I shall not dwell here on the period in his life from his appointment as metropolitan to the outbreak of the war. I would like to mention, however, that the Uniate Catholic church, he and his entourage, suffered a great deal in the first period of World War II. He often related to me the story of Soviet persecutions and harassments which lasted form 1939 until the outbreak of the war between Germany and the Soviet Union. In any event, the period of interest to us began on June 22, 1941.

The Ukrainians were overjoyed by the entry of German troops into Lvov and prepared a tumultuous welcome for the new rulers. They saw them as liberators from the Soviet occupation, believing that the Germans would grant them complete independence and allow them to build an independent Ukraine. They were in for a bitter disappointment.

On June 30, 1941, the O.U.N. (Organization of Ukrainian Nationalists) proclaimed the establishment of an independent Ukraine and the establishment of a Ukrainian government headed by Yaroslav Stetsko. The leader of this organization, founded in 1929, was Konovalets. He was murdered in 1938 and Andrey Melnyk was elected as the wartime chairman. In 1940 the organization split into two independent bodies: the original O.U.N. led by Melnyk and an extreme revolutionary organization led by Stefan Bandera.

The proclamation of Ukrainian independence was not at all to the Germans' liking. Several days later Bandera and the entire Ukrainian leadership were rounded up and sent to a concentration camp.

Of unique interest to Jews is a pastoral letter issued by Metropolitan Sheptytskyi on July 1, 1941, shortly after the proclamation of Ukrainian independence. In his letter the metropolitan called upon the Ukrainian people to display obedience and discipline and to comply with the instructions of the new government. He expected the new government, or rather demanded it, to issue instructions and enact laws founded on justice, which would ensure the well-being and welfare of all residents of the land, regardless of religious faith, national allegiance, or social status.

This particular passage in the metropolitan's letter, important as it was to Jews, tells us something about its author. In those crazy days, speaking publicly about the duty of tolerance toward other religions, by which the metropolitan implicitly meant Jews, required a great deal of courage and an unshakable commitment to moral principles. It is to be remembered that at that time massacres of Jews were proceeding apace with Ukrainians unfortunately taking part in them.

An appeal of this sort was extremely unpopular and entailed grave risk for its proponent. And, in fact, the consequences were not late in coming. Himmler called for the metropolitan's arrest. He immediately issued orders to the governor of Lvov, Lasch, and, if I remember correctly, to the head of the Gestapo in the city to arrest the metropolitan forthwith. In response Lasch submitted a detailed report on the situation. He stressed that the metropolitan's arrest was likely to provoke the undying hostility of the Ukrainian population on whose support the Germans must rely at present. The local Ukrainian population, he said, had been the only ally of the Germans in their military operations in eastern Galicia and remained such also in those parts of the Ukraine that were being overrun at the present time. The metropolitan enjoyed immense popularity and his arrest could jeopardize the security of the entire German army operating in the area. Himmler backed down on the arrest but ordered that the metropolitan be closely watched and all his movements followed.

According to Ukrainian clerical circles, the German stance toward the metropolitan and the proclamation of an independent Ukrainian government opened a rift between the Ukrainian population and the Germans and aroused hostility toward the German army. These circles also argued that Germany was defeated on Ukrainian soil because the Germans succeeded in overrunning only a small part of the Russian territory. The German defeat in the Ukraine was to be attributed to the hostile attitude on the part of the Ukrainian population. These views were held by the Ukrainians in the metropolitan's palace and throughout his archbishopric.

In actual fact, Hitler divided the Ukraine into two parts. Eastern Galicia, i.e. the western Ukraine, was incorporated into the General Government, whereas the remaining part of the country was placed under the rule of *Reichskommissar* Koch who did his utmost to gain the sympathy of the Ukrainians by persecuting other national groups living there.

The crimes committed by *Reichskommissar* Koch and the Nazi rulers in the Ukraine are sufficiently known. In addition, many Ukrainians took an active part in the persecutions and massacres of Jews.

To resume my narrative: I was accommodated in the metropolitan's library. A monk who was the metropolitan's personal attendant brought me meals three times a day. My food consisted mostly of bread, vegetables, and sometimes a boiled egg or milk. All this was not brought from the kitchen, as my stay in the palace was a closely guarded secret. Only two people knew about me: this monk and the metropolitan's secretary, Father Hrtzai. The latter, an intelligent and good-humored man, was very friendly to me, displayed a warm-hearted attitude toward the Jews, and commiserated with them in their tragedy.

On the second day after my arrival at the palace I was paid a visit by Abbot Kliment Sheptytskyi. He sat with me for several hours in my corner in the library, comforted me, and brought me greetings from my wife and daughter. For reasons of security he refused to reveal their hiding place. In these times of ordeal, he said, no one knows what the day will bring. One of us could fall into the hands of the Gestapo and under torture disclose the hiding place. For the time being it was enough to know that they were healthy and safe. My wife was furnished with good Ukrainian papers and worked outside, whereas the child was placed in a children's home. His soft, soothing words did not fit at all with his stern, ascetic countenance. I felt he was doing his utmost to empathize with and comprehend the unspeakable tragedy of me and my people. He commiserated with us and shared our torments. On one occasion he promised me, on his own and the metropolitan's behalf, to do everything possible to save Jewish children. "I must say, however," he added, "that this is a very difficult undertaking. Not everyone has risen to such a degree of devotion as to risk his life to save Jews. Not everyone was brought up in this way. It is easier to save girls than boys. The metropolitan issued instructions to certain priests in district towns on how to rescue children and where to bring them. But I shall not call them by name, again for reasons of security."

The Monastery

I stayed in the metropolitan's library on Jura Mountain through June 1, 1943. On the night of June 2, Hrtzai informed me that that very night I would have to leave the palace and move to the Studite monastery at Piotr Skarga Street. It was not safe for me to stay on Jura Mountain. There were too many people, including Germans, coming on business to the palace, which was the center of the Uniate Catholic church. I would be much safer behind the walls of a peaceful, quiet Studite monastery which was seldom visited by outsiders. I would also feel safer and therefore it would be easier for me to endure the times of ordeal, the nightmare of wartime.

Late at night Hrtzai entered the library in the company of a middle-aged monk and introduced him to me: "This is Brother Teodosy, a monk of the Studite monastery. He will be your escort, companion, and intermediary in your contacts with the outside world."

I could not see his face in the darkness, but I heard his soft, friendly voice and felt the touch of his work-coarsened hand.

"My name is Teodosy. I am the emissary of His Holiness the Metropolitan. From now on I will take care of you."

He dressed me in a long robe and covered my head with the tall hood of the Studites. Holding my hand he led me out of the palace. Before setting out we stopped at the gate and he said: "It is possible that we will be stopped and checked on the way. These are times of fear. You must know this: Your name is Brother Mateusz. All your papers are with the abbot. Should they ask you where you are coming from, you will say that you brought books from the monastery library to the metropolitan and now you are returning to the monastery. But in principle I will do the talking. Your command of Ukrainian is not fluent enough and it is better that I speak for both of us. Try to refrain from speaking as much as possible."

The gate swung open. Holding my hand, he led me outside. We entered a small and narrow alley that led straight from Jura Mountain to Piotr Skanga Street.

We arrived at a large building stretching the length of the small alley. On the right was a modern hospital bearing the metropolitan's name, which he founded to provide medical services to the Ukrainian population. The monastery was to the left. Beyond the street was Jura Mountain, the cathedral, the theological seminary, and the metro-politan's palace. The windows of the monastery and the hospital faced Jura Mountain.

We stopped before the gate. Brother Teodosy rang the bell three times as agreed upon and the gate was opened by the abbot himself. He was a tall thin man with an ascetic face and he wore the black robes of a monk. He had been waiting for me. He greeted me and led me to a small room on the third floor at the end of the hallway, right by the staircase leading to the attic. He addressed me by my assumed name:

"Atach Matey (Brother Mateusz), for the time being you shall remain in this cell. Brother Teodosy will provide for all your needs. You must not leave the cell. With the exception of myself, Brother Teodosy, and another young brother, a student at the theological seminary whose name is Ben, no one knows of your being here."

Thereupon they locked me in the cell and left. The cell was lit by an electric light bulb and contained a sleeping board, a small table, and a chair. A jug of water and pewter cup stood in the corner.

I lay down on the sleeping board and started thinking. For the first time since my escape from the camp I tried to assess my new and strange situation. Until that moment in the cell I was acting as if in a dream. Although I had been conscious of my actions and whereabouts, my mind was simply incapable of absorbing the radical change in my situation. The difference between these two worlds, the Janowski camp and its nightmare, its atrocities and murders, on the one hand, and the quiet and stillness of the shut-off and isolated monastery, was too great.

What were the Jews doing now in the ghetto? I kept wondering. What was going on there? What happened to my friends in the camp? It was clear to me that something was wrong. I was plagued by remorse. Did I have the right to escape and save myself? The frightening stillness of the locked cell reverberated in my head. I could neither rest nor sleep.

Wild scenes from my life in the camp danced before my eyes as if in a kaleidoscope. I recalled the note that my wife had sent me through a prisoner whom I did not know. In her note she intimated that a refuge was waiting for me at Sheptytskyi's residence, which meant that I could escape without fear. A shelter was ready for me. The note meant life, whereas each day in the camp meant death. Everyone of us wanted so much to live, to live at any price, to live as a free man and see Hitler's defeat.

I can hardly find the words to describe the inner struggle that raged in my heart on the cold winter morning during the roll call. I think that without having gone through the experience of a forced labor camp, one simply cannot understand this inner life-and-death struggle. To me it seemed then that in my hand I was holding a burning flame and not a written note from my wife. And I decided to let the opportunity pass. I did not even tell my friends about it. I knew full well that for every escaped prisoner four or five other Jews would be shot at the next roll call. This consideration was of crucial importance in my decision. Escape under these circumstances runs counter to Jewish morality and law. So I stayed on. "Why should you regard your blood as more red [of better quality] than the blood of others and your life as more worthy than the life of others? Perhaps the opposite is true?" (Treatise Sanhedrin, 74b).

But what about the present? I was told about the slaughter in the camp by the Polish manager of the VIB factory at Zamarstynowska Street at eleven o'clock in the morning, after the night shift. All one hundred prisoners from that shift fled. Should I have stayed and returned to the camp alone? Whom would I have helped by returning to the camp? What good would it have done? I decided to escape.

And now I am here in an isolated cell in a Ukrainian monastery. So strange, almost like a dream, but true nonetheless. Never in my life had I had as much as an inkling that one day I would find refuge in a Ukrainian monastery. My heart was beating madly and my temples throbbed with pain.

I tried to comprehend my situation, the situation of a man turned hunted beast seeking some hiding place, and the horrendous predicament of my people in all its acuteness. My lips whispered the words of the great mourner in the Book of Lamentations (2:19–20):

> Arise, cry out in the night; in the beginning of the watches pour out thy heart like water before the face of the Lord: lift up thy hands toward Him for the life of thy young ones, that faint for hunger in the top of every street.
> Behold, O Lord, and consider to whom Thou hast done this.

The monastery was asleep and quiet. I was unable to sleep and kept turning on my sleeping board. The dawn broke. Bright rays of the new day began filtering through the small window of my cell. At a distance I heard the creak of doors and human steps.

In the grayness of dawn I heard the knocks of a wooden clapper: one of the monks was waking the other monks for the morning prayer. He passed through all the hallways, knocked with his clapper and sang something with a monotonous voice. At first I couldn't catch his words. But as he drew near my cell I understood. He was waking the monks with a verse from Psalm 134:

> Behold, bless ye the Lord, all ye servants of the Lord,
> Which by night stand in the house of the Lord.
> Lift up your hands in the sanctuary, and bless the Lord.

I recognized the Old Church Slavonic language, which I had learned in my days at Vienna University. I was interested in the language then and studied it with Professor Trubetskoy, a Russian prince and a scholar who had escaped from Russia during the Revolution and was offered the chair of Slavic studies at Vienna University.

Presently all the floors and hallways of the monastery were abuzz with activity. The monks washed and made preparations for the morning prayer in the great chapel situated in a large spacious chamber on the ground floor.

The sounds of commotion soon died down and deep stillness again enveloped the monastery. Now and then I could hear the chants, the monks' prayers.

The light grew stronger by the minute and the new day was born. I got out of bed and washed my hands and my burning face in the water from the jug. My meager satchel containing a few belongings lay next to the sleeping board. I looked for the prayer shawl and phylacteries I had with me in the camp. Even in the most difficult and dangerous moments I never parted from them. This time, however, I did not find them in my satchel. One day later, after I got a bit used to my new surroundings, I summoned the courage to ask Brother Teodosy about the little sack with my religious articles. Teodosy told me he had asked the abbot what to do with the sack and whether it should be returned to me. Having given this matter serious thought they decided to remove the sack and hide it away.

"These are stormy and dangerous times. We are never exempt from search. If the Gestapo finds a bundle with a Jewish prayer shawl and phylacteries, this would expose the entire monastery, not to mention your life, to great danger. If, with God's help, we are able to save you and you survive the war, we shall return them to you."

I accepted this explanation and did not press anymore.

I spent two days in the cell. On June 4, late at night, the door opened softly and the abbot, together with Brother Teodosy and the young theology student Ben, entered my cell. They seated themselves on my sleeping board and said the following:

"There is a great tension in the city. Rumors abound about a terrible and dreadful *Aktion*. People talk about the total liquidation of the camp and the ghetto. The Aryan residents are warned not to shelter Jews under pain of death. The Germans are conducting searches in private houses, public buildings, and monasteries. We cannot be certain that they will not search our monastery too. We therefore consulted with the metropolitan and decided to find you a more secure accommodation in the attic of our monastery. For this purpose we have brought a skilled carpenter from the monastery in Liczakow; the metropolitan himself made him privy to our secret and asked him to prepare a concealed hiding place for you in the attic. Three of us helped him with his work and no one except us knows about the hiding place. Now we must move you there."

I realized that my situation had taken a turn for the worse. I gathered my bundle and was ready to go wherever they took me. In such moments you do not ask questions; you do as you are told.

Teodosy put out his lamp, softly opened the door and left first. After five minutes we heard the creak of a door being opened. We left the cell and with soft steps began ascending the stairs leading to the attic. The iron door leading to the attic was open.

In the attic Brother Teodosy lit my way with a small electric lamp. The large and spacious attic was divided into sections by wooden partitions. Teodosy stopped next to one of them, cautiously slid several boards, and pointed to the opening of my hiding place. I bent and crawled inside. I saw a bed with wire netting without a mattress. There were several weathered peasant coats lying on the bed.

"You will sleep here," he said. "We did not bring a mattress and bedding on purpose in case of a search. For the time being, you will have to make do with what we've brought." They wished me good night and left.

I remained in the darkness of my hideout, prey to my thoughts. Slowly my eyes accustomed themselves to the darkness and I was able to survey my surroundings.

My hideout was the size of an average room. The attic was roofed with sheet iron. There were two small windows. It was so cold my body was trembling. I lay on the bed and covered myself with the old coats. I didn't feel the hard wire netting of the bed and slept like a rock.

When I awoke my hideout was awash with light. I got out of bed, stretched my hurting, frozen limbs, and approached the window. I opened it and let my body bask in the warm rays of the rising sun. It was a crystal clear, bright June morning. I could see the green and brightly illuminated Jura Mountain. It was early summer. The frame of my window allowed a full view of Jura Mountain and a small section of Tokarzewski Street. The city was slowly stirring with life and getting ready for the day's work.

I drew away from the window facing east and approached the second, western window. The weathered and filthy houses of Szumlanska Street rose up toward me as though from the depths of a ravine.

On both sides of the attic I watched people slowly leaving their homes, as if still weighed down by sleep. They were going to work, to bolster the German war effort. The world was not going to stop because of the destruction of several hundred thousand Jews. The city carried on with its daily routine.

I spent all summer from June 4, 1943, until September 1943 in my hideout.

The first week was difficult, perhaps the most tragic during this period. The liquidation of the ghetto took place in early June. Throughout the week I heard shouts, screams, gunshots. The nights of the middle of June etched themselves deeply in my memory. Time and again I was woken in the middle of the night by weeping, crying, and heartrending voices of hunted Jews flushed out of their hiding places in the district where the monastery was located. My heart felt the torments of the Jews going to their death, and I languished in pain and powerlessness. No written word can convey these torments.

Throughout June Brother Teodosy sneaked softly into my room once a day or every other day, bringing food, water, and now and then also the Ukrainian newspaper *Ukrainski Visti*. He was pale with fear and pain. I could see that he was deeply anguished by the events in the ghetto.

From him I learned the first details about the liquidation of the Lvov ghetto. Any Jew attempting resistance was shot on the spot. Transports of children presented a truly horrendous and hair-raising spectacle. Both dead and alive, scared to death and shot to death, with crushed skulls, all of them were transported in the same cart to the Kleparow train station and the Janowski camp. Transports to the camp were rolling day and night.

In the camp itself selection took place. The young and strong were allowed to live for the time being. All the older and elderly people were shipped off to Belzec.

Teodosy also told me about the attempt at armed resistance in the ghetto. In the city people relished recounting the story of a bunker at Lokietek Street that had been holding out for several days, which the Germans had not yet succeeded in overcoming. The Germans deployed Ukrainian policemen against the bunker, which explains how the news reached me.

One week later I came across official confirmation of the story. In a mid-June issue of the newspaper *Lvivski Visti* I found a large obituary notice telling the story of a Ukrainian policeman who fell in the battle with the Jewish "bandits" in the Lvov ghetto. He was described as "killed by a bullet of a murderous Jew." It goes without saying that the policeman was given a lavish funeral and that his coffin was carried by representatives of various public institutions and organizations. The Germans organized the funeral and were among the chief speakers. In short, the policeman was paid his last respects with great fanfare.

How hypocritical, unfounded, and meaningless were the attacks launched for hundreds of years by Aryan Christendom against the revengeful Jews, against their avenging God. The obituary notice in the Ukrainian newspaper tore the veil of hypocrisy off these shameless faces. No, I was not at all embarrassed by the verse "the God of revenge is the Lord."

The Ukrainian paper was like a balm on my pained heart. From now on it can be said that Jews were defending themselves and a policeman was killed in the battle with them. The Jews of the Lvov ghetto dared to take up arms against their oppressors, dared to resist and take revenge.

The month of June passed. Lvov had been declared *Judenrein*. The ghetto ruins remained like a tombstone testifying to the last fateful struggle. And I was still stuck in my hideout.

As I said, the attic was roofed with sheet iron. On hot days the iron absorbed the heat and many times I was close to fainting. Nights were cold and sent shivers through my body. In the night the sheet iron would soon lose the heat of the day: "During the day I was consumed by scorching heat, and by ice during the night." I never understood better the meaning of this verse than during my stay in the Studite monastery.

My only reading material consisted of the aforementioned Ukrainian newspaper, the Bible, and the New Testament in Delitzsch's translation.

My food was brought either by Teodosy or by the young theology student Ben. They did not spend much time with me and refrained from conversation. The Aryan city residents lived in constant fear, particularly those who sheltered Jews in their homes. Upon discovery of such a hideout the Germans executed both the hiding Jews and their protectors.

Days and nights in my hideout. Long, hot days, without news from the outside world, without spiritual nourishment. For hours on end I stood by the window watching God's world. On one side, Jura Mountain bathed in the glory of green, succulent colors. On the other side, the street and houses swarming with men, women, and children. From the bottom of my heart I poured my fervent prayer before the Throne of Glory: "Master of the world, why? Why are all these people down there allowed to walk as they please, whereas I languish here in this solitary cell?" I don't think there was a person in the world capable of describing or empathizing with the feelings of a Jew in those days, as he stood by the window and looked out on the world created by God. On more than one occasion I was close to going insane, as I thought I might be the only Jew left in the world. In such moments I found consolation in prayer and the Book of Psalms, the psalms that for thousands of years had been comforting Jews in dire straits. In a whisper my lips poured forth bitter complaints before the great, merciful, yet inexplicable God. Having emptied my heart of its bitterness and poured out my anguish before the Master of the world, I was able to calm myself for a little while.

The street with its clamor, its passersby, its orderly, undisturbed, daily routine, was driving me crazy. Whenever I looked out of the window I was close to losing my mind. Women pushing prams with babies in them, elderly men seated comfortably on benches and chatting at leisure, a young couple in embrace strolling at their leisure down the street, a group of children singing, their innocent faces radiant with joy. Master of the world? How is this possible? Don't they know what is going on across the fence? Don't they know the blood flows there like water and people are being burned alive?

The things I observed daily from the attic window and my mute powerless pain conspired to demolish all foundations of faith in human beings. Jew hatred was out for everyone to see. The rift seemed too wide to ever be healed. Our sages said: Halakah determined that Esau hates Jacob. This intense hatred hangs over us like a cruel verdict, a merciless decree. Nothing in the world, not even the rivers of Jewish blood, seems capable of extinguishing this hatred.

I recall an incident that took place on Jura Mountain in the middle of August which I witnessed from my hideout in the monastery. It was Sunday afternoon. Dozens of people who lived near the mountain were stretched out on the grass among the trees. Some families spread blankets to have a picnic in the park. People were vacationing after a week of heavy work. Suddenly I saw a boy, twelve, perhaps fourteen years old, walking toward the mountain with hesitant steps. He stopped often, looking around him, probably searching for a place to sit. After a while he started walking faster, ascended the slope and seated himself under a low but expansive tree, some distance away from the other vacationers. From the first moment the boy captured my attention. I didn't like his nervous stride and the isolated spot he chose under the tree. He made me suspicious that he was Jewish. From where I stood I could only discern the contours of his face but could not make out the details. One thing I saw clearly: the movement of his eyes, the nervous glances, the looks over his shoulder. I could not see the color of his eyes, but I saw their restlessness and the terrible fear I knew so well. Right away I felt the invisible thread of sympathy binding me to the boy. I stood by the window and watched him as if hypnotized. He leaned his head against the tree. Perhaps he was asleep, or just resting and surveying his surroundings? Who knows what goes on in the mind of a hunted Jewish boy?

I stood glued to the window for over an hour. It was six, perhaps seven in the evening; the summer dusk descended slowly. Then a group of screaming children appeared on the mountain. They scattered round about. Everything was as it should be: happy children at play, screaming and filling the air with noise. Nothing out of the ordinary.

Chasing each other, two children drew close to the tree under which the boy was resting. They stopped and looked at him. One of them approached him and seemed to ask him something. I could not hear a thing. But I saw the second boy running like a released arrow back to other children and with visible agitation pointing at the boy and the child standing next to him. Shortly thereafter the whole group walked to the tree and surrounded the boy. The glances and conversation lasted about five minutes. I understood they were engaged in an agitated argument. The voices reached the ears of the adults picnicking on the grass. Some of them got up and walked to the boy under the tree. The children drew away and the adults started interrogating the boy, speaking with many voices and waving hands. Suddenly the entire mountain was astir and everyone became agitated. With the appearance of a Ukrainian policeman the tension reached its peak. I had no way of knowing whether they summoned the policeman or he just happened to be there. In any event, he walked up to the boy. The crowd retreated. The policeman's investigation was short. Several minutes later I saw him leading the boy by the hand to Grodecka Street.

I strained my eyes in an effort to see the boy's face; perhaps it could tell me something about what was going on in his mind. I could not see his face but I was able to discern that his insecurity and nervousness were gone. He walked calmly by the side of the Ukrainian policeman.

Then, in a flash of recognition, I understood; it was resignation, the unmistakable sign of resignation. All Jews, having crossed the threshold of fear and anxiety, looked like that. Resigned, even apathetic, they walked to their death.

The boy was gone and night had fallen. Slowly people began leaving Jura Mountain. I remained alone with my thoughts. Then I saw myself as a five- or six-year-old-boy in the heder of my native town of Grzymalow. We were studying the chapter on the sacrifice of Isaac. I was deeply moved by this interesting, simple, yet powerful story. Our rabbi knew how to tell the story well: Abraham, our father, leads his only son to be sacrificed. Behold, they have already reached the top of Mount Moriah. Behold, Abraham binds the little Isaac, lays him on the altar, and raises the knife to slaughter his only son.

My nerves could not withstand the tension of the story and I broke into a cry. Rabbi David Hantzis, his white beard spread profusely over his chest, leans over me, caresses me with his silky hand and says in a soothing voice: "Hush, my child, hush, don't cry, this is just a trial. The angel from heaven betook himself to earth, came, and saved Isaac."

O, Lord! Where is the angel to save our children from the sacrifice?

Next morning Brother Teodosy came to my cell. He closed the door softly and sat down. I could see he wanted to tell me something. We were both silent for a long while. I broke the silence and asked him whether he knew what had taken place yesterday on the mountain. He replied as follows:

"We are all greatly distressed by what happened yesterday. The crowd handed over a Jewish boy to the police. It seems that the child had escaped from the Gestapo men who had uncovered the bunker of his family." Teodosy stopped for a moment and went on: "Not all the people behave as did those yesterday on the mountain. I have not told you this until now, but I can see the grief on your face and I wish to tell you something. I and my friend, Brother Lazar, work as cobblers in the 'Solid' factory. In the factory's cellar, we constructed a bunker where we hide a Jewish family by the name of Funk. I pray to God, that we will succeed in saving them. And do you think it is easy to hide you in this monastery? Several weeks after you were brought here, the searches for hiding Jews intensified. The abbot, Father Nikanor, convened all the brothers and revealed to them the secret of your being here. Should the Germans search the place and find you, we must take steps to remove any suspicion from the monastery and forestall the possibility of being charged with collective responsibility for this act. Only in this way can the monastery be saved from destruction and the monks from death. Thus one of the monks must volunteer to assume personal responsibility. At that moment the abbot asked the gathering: 'Who is willing to take the responsibility upon himself?' Everyone stepped forward like one man. Everyone was willing to take the risk. And you must know that not only we, who remain under the personal influence of Metropolitan Sheptytskyi, but also a number of clergymen from district towns enlisted themselves in the campaign of rescuing Jews, particularly Jewish children. The names include Kotiv, Ivanyuk, Mark Stek, Titus Prostyuk, Hrtzai, Martinyuk, Cyprian, the Abbess of the Studite convent Iosefa, Herman Budzinsky, and others."

Kind Teodosy, this noble soul realized how greatly I was distressed by the incident of the day before and therefore sought to comfort me. He sat in my hideout for a long time, told me the story of his life and about his work. When he left, my abode was completely dark.

Again I returned to my thoughts. How difficult it is to reconcile the two sections of the Ukrainian people. On one hand, all the national Ukrainian heroes (Khmelnytskyi, Nalivoyka, Gontar, and, last but not least, Petlyura, as well as the present Ukrainian police assisting the Germans in the destruction of the Jewish people) and every national reawakening or uprising were always connected with spilling rivers of Jewish blood. The Ukrainians have always vented their wrath against the Jews. On the other hand, there are the noble figures of the metropolitan, his brother the abbot, the monks and priests Titus, Hrtzai, Stek, Martinyuk, and others. How is this possible? How can one reconcile these two opposites?

The month of August was drawing to an end and September was knocking on the door. Cooler nights announced the approach of autumn. Teodosy continued to visit and bring me news from the outside world: here a Jewish bunker was discovered in the ghetto; there the peasants staged a raid, caught several dozen Jews hiding in the woods, and handed them over to the Gestapo. There was only one piece of good news: the German front was cracking and heading toward collapse. All signs indicated imminent defeat.

One night in the middle of September, I heard a suspicious noise in the hallways of the monastery. Actually I sensed it rather than heard it. Probably my overwrought nerves helped my already overly developed sense of hearing. Then I heard the characteristic sound of heavy steps on the staircase leading to the attic. The lock creaked and the iron door opened. Now I could distinctly hear the conversation between Abbot

Nikanor and his German guests. The search! It didn't matter what or whom they were searching for. If they discovered my concealed hideout, I was as good as gone. My body was shivering, my heart thumped and beat like mad. My eyes darted about in the darkness, searching for a place to hide. Where could I hide? I kept hearing the steps and loud voices. They were looking for something, I was certain. Then I heard them right next to my hideout. In a moment they would remove the sliding boards and seal my fate.

Then Providence decreed otherwise. The search in the attic lasted ten minutes, but for me it was an eternity. A heavy load lifted from my heart when I heard the creak of the closing door. I was saved. The hideout was well concealed. Praise to you, O mighty God.

Impatiently I waited for the new day. Teodosy would certainly tell me what happened and the reason for the search. But Teodosy did not appear. I kept waiting in vain. My impatience and restlessness mounted with the coming of the night.

Back in the Metropolitan's Palace

At about eleven o'clock at night I was given another scare. The iron door was opened and a man started walking softly toward my hideout and removed the sliding boards. It was Ben. He was excited and scared. He told me that someone must have informed the Germans and last night they conducted a thorough search of the premises. They turned everything upside down: the monks' cells, the library, the large refectory, the secretariat, and they even searched in the chapel. Finally, they demanded the keys to the attic, but fortunately didn't find anything. All ended well. However the metropolitan had decided to transfer me back to his palace. He was afraid of the Gestapo and did not trust them. So that night Teodosy would take me back to Jura Mountain.

I listened to the news with equanimity. I had always been ready for departure, for any fresh trouble, ready to adjust myself to any new situation. Now, awake, I waited for Teodosy to take me with him.

He came at midnight and brought some clothes. He told me about our route and, the main thing, handed me a document issued by the monastery stating my identity as Brother Mateusz. If we are checked, I am a monk and my name is Mateusz. It reminded me of all the precautions we had taken in early summer during my transfer from the palace to Piotr Skarga Street.

Several minutes later we were outside. I inhaled deeply the cool, fresh night air, which nearly intoxicated me after my long confinement in the attic. Teodosy walked quickly and I dragged myself behind him with difficulty. During the past summer I hadn't had much opportunity to walk and apparently was out of practice. No one intercepted us on the way to the palace.

The gate opened instantly after we rang the bell. A monk was waiting for us. Teodosy attended to everything.

A few moments later I found myself again in the concealed corner of the library where I had hidden at the beginning of summer. I seated myself on the by-now-familiar lounge chair and immediately fell prey to my thoughts. I keep moving on, I thought, like the Wandering Jew. But this is not the curse that pursues me, nor the wrath of God. People, evil, accursed people haunt me. I am like an animal in the forest, trying to hide from the hunter's bullet. As it happened I found protection and help in the palace of a Christian archbishop, in fact, in the residence of a Ukrainian archbishop, whose people, as servants of the German master, take part in the extermination of Jews. That I should find some security here of all places seems like a trick that fate played on me.

Father Kotiv came to see me in the morning, bringing me a short note from my wife. She and the child are well and hope to gain freedom soon. Although I still didn't know their whereabouts, at least this information comforted me.

I was also visited by Abbot Kliment, Hrtzai, and Teodosy. The abbot was moved to tears. He gave me his solemn assurance that all the people and children under his protection were alive, well, and well hidden, and that nothing untoward would happen to them. Before leaving he informed me that in the evening he would take me to the metropolitan.

At 9:00 P.M. Hrtzai came to my hideout; I think he served as the metropolitan's personal secretary. He took me to the first floor and ushered me without delay into the workroom of the metropolitan.

Half-paralyzed, Sheptytskyi was in his chair, dressed in a long dark robe with a leather belt. His thick, long, white beard outlined, as if with the brush strokes of a master painter, his delicate features, which radiated spirituality and humanity. He gave me his hand, greeted me with Shalom in Hebrew, and asked me to sit next to him. The hearing of this over eighty-year-old man was impaired. Hrtzai left and we remained alone. Neither of us spoke. I could feel that the subject he wanted to talk about could not easily be broached. Finally, he asked me to give him a truthful account of the Janowski camp. He had reliable information about the situation in the Lvov ghetto and the ghettos in the cities and small towns of the region. In contrast, the news reaching him from the camp was unclear and frightening. He expressed his wish to hear an eyewitness account.

I complied with his wish. Until late at night I recounted the sanguinary tale of the Janowski camp. I described the hellfire raging there and the deeds of the archhenchmen: Willhaus, Epler, Gebauer, Blum, Heinisch, Heinin, Grzymek, and others.

The metropolitan broke down. Now and then he wiped a tear rolling down his cheek. He was moved to the bottom of his heart. Parting from me he gave me the full text of his letter to Himmler, as well as his pastoral letter published in Ukrainian under the title "Thou shall not murder" in *Lvivski Archeparkhialni Vidomosti* (50, no. 11 [Nov. 1942]: 177–83; see Appendix 3). With these two documents in hand I retired to my hiding place in the library.

I began reading the two works the next morning. Since the metropolitan had told me about them at our first meeting, I knew of their existence. But this time it was different. It was the aftermath of the liquidation of the ghetto; the burning flames had not yet died down and Jewish existence had been so thoroughly obliterated that it seemed not a single Jew in Europe would survive the disaster and Jewry would be erased from the face of the earth. Against this background the pastoral letter of Metropolitan Sheptytskyi carried special significance. It also reflected the extraordinary humanity and moral authority of its author.

The two letters left a powerful impression on me. In his letter to Himmler the metropolitan called on him to remove Ukrainian policemen from all extermination operations carried out against the Jews. The ordinary Ukrainian is crude and in the future he would likely do to his countrymen, his brethren, what he had done to the Jews. He becomes inured to murder and it would be difficult for him to unlearn it.

The pastoral letter revealed a deeply humanistic outlook. I was confused. I saw the hatred harbored by the Ukrainian people, the atrocities perpetrated by its policemen, the collaboration of the Ukrainian intelligentsia with the Germans. And now I read the noble-minded, uncompromising document drawn up by the metropolitan and his aides.

Again I tried to come to grips with these two contradictory aspects of the same people. I was alone and had no one with whom to share and exchange views, to share my doubts, to soothe my nerves. I must struggle alone and keep silent.

Several days later Father Hrtzai brought me a number of books containing accounts of travel to the Land of Israel, mostly memoirs or diaries of pilgrims who traveled there at various times. In several of them I found descriptions of the Zionist venture and Jewish settlement in the Land of Israel such as the book of travels by Bishop Slipyi. At the same time, however, I must say that not one of these books was overly sympathetic to Jewry, particularly to the new community in the Land of Israel.

Hrtzai recommended one book in particular, describing the pilgrimage the metropolitan made in 1903 at the head of a large group of priests and laymen. The book, entitled *When the Russians Went in the Footsteps of Daniella,* was written on the instructions of the metropolitan by one of the priests who participated in the journey. Daniella, a Russian Slav who lived in the early Middle Ages, was one of the founders of the Ukrainian people. He made a pilgrimage to the Holy Land and described his journey in a book written in Old Church Slavonic. The author of the present book painted in vivid colors the holy places visited by the metropolitan and his fellow pilgrims. A whole chapter was devoted to the history of the Temple and the Western Wall. In particular, he described the deep impression left on him by a large group of Jews who prayed with great devotion and fervor by the Wall, weeping over the destruction of the Temple. This scene seems to have left a deep impression. He writes: "How vastly different were these Jews weeping at the ancient wall from our Jewish merchants plying their trade in the cities and towns of eastern Galicia." The author's sympathy was clearly with the picturesque group of Jews weeping at the Western Wall, or as he called it the "Wailing Wall." He concluded this chapter with these words: "My heart goes out to you, weeping Jews, forever you will weep and will not stop, the walls will never be rebuilt. For this is what heaven has ordained."

All the books that Hrtzai brought to me were written more or less in this vein. Obviously the priest wished to comfort me with accounts of the Land of Israel which he knew was close to my heart. He could not surmise that these descriptions caused me great distress and even aggravated my torment.

Needless to say, I could not discuss this with Hrtzai. But to me the reflections of the Ukrainian priest as he stood by the Western Wall contained in a nutshell the persistent, two-thousand-year-old controversy between Judaism and Christianity. To make matters even more complicated, I was living in a stronghold of Christians who had saved me and my loved ones from death. How could I argue with them?

Several days later I had another opportunity to visit the metropolitan in his workroom. At the sight of the patriarchal visage of the man and his kind eyes, I summoned my courage and made up my mind to ask him about the underlying meaning of the pilgrimage book. Did the reflections of this Ukrainian priest lead to the conclusion that the Christian church does not believe in an independent Jewish community in the Land of Israel and will refuse to recognize it?

The metropolitan thought for a moment before answering and then began: "I would like to place your question in the context of the present situation of the people of Israel. You must know that the Church displays a humane and friendly attitude toward the Jewish people. The official Church harshly and sternly denounces attacks on Jews. We are opposed to the atrocities of the Nazis and we shall do our utmost to denounce them as inhuman and sacrilegious. The pastoral letter of the German cardinal Faulhaber, as well as my own pastoral letter of November 1942, provide unmistakable evidence of the stance of the Church toward Nazism and its position on the Jewish question. Publication of my pastoral letter was beset with difficulties and it had to pass through several trials of censorship. Recently an official delegation from the German Foreign Ministry paid me a visit. I openly denounced their deeds and lodged a protest against the brutal and cruel treatment of the Jews. As human beings we are obliged to voice our opposition to this and condemn in the strongest terms the persecution of Jews and all forms of racial discrimination. I am aware that over the centuries Christendom committed sins against the Jews. I am aggrieved by this, deeply aggrieved, and I do as much as I can to forestall the grave sin of persecution of Jews. This much I stressed in my letter to Himmler. As for the book on the pilgrimage, there are a number of theological postulations of a dogmatic nature which require us to take certain exceptions to the Zionist political aspirations concerning an independent Jewish state in Palestine."

The metropolitan fell silent for a moment and continued: "Have you ever thought about it and asked yourself, what is the source of the hatred and savage persecution of the Jewish people from ancient times until the present? What is their origin?" He pointed at the bookshelves, asked me to find the New Testament in Hebrew translation and locate chapter 27, verse 25 in the Gospel according to Matthew: "It says there 'And the whole people answered and said His blood will be on us and on our children.' In other places Jesus says explicitly that not a stone will be left standing of the Temple and the glory of Jerusalem. If you ponder this and take into consideration the relevant chapters in the New

Testament, you will understand the comments of the author of the book on our pilgrimage."

Needless to say, I did not argue with him. For how could I enter into an argument with him about the reasons for Jew-hatred and the persistent persecutions, I, a Jew who had found sanctuary in the palace of the prince of the Church, a fugitive from the Janowski camp, hunted like a wild beast by his oppressors?

He let the matter rest at that and began telling me how every year on the eve of Passover he used to send a considerable donation to the poor in the various communities of eastern Galicia to buy flour for matzoth. The bulk of the money went to the community of Lvov and Podhajce. The rabbi of Podhajce, Rabbi Lilienfeld, was on very friendly terms with the Sheptytskyi family. He also told me that his teacher of the Hebrew language and modern Hebrew literature was the antiquarian book dealer and scholar Siegel. The metropolitan had begun his study of Hebrew at the theological seminary. He wrote his letters to Jewish communities in Hebrew and emphasized that the Passover alms were designated for the poor in accordance with the age-old Jewish custom in the lands of the Diaspora.

At noon the next day Father Hrtzai informed me that the metropolitan wished to see me again that evening.

For reasons of security the metropolitan used to see me at night after all the guests and visitors on business were gone.

Just before nine o'clock in the evening Hrtzai ushered me into the metropolitan's workroom and left us alone. I remained standing but the metropolitan motioned to me with his half-paralyzed hand to draw near him and sit in the chair next to his.

"Our conversation yesterday did not let me sleep. I am remorseful and sorry about the content of our conversation. I shouldn't have spoken as I did. In the ongoing ordeal, when the Jewish people bleed to death and sacrifice hundreds of thousands of innocent victims, I should have known better than to touch upon this subject. I knew that such a conversation aggrieved you greatly. I ask you to forgive me. After all I am mortal and for a moment I let myself be distracted."

He reached out his hand and warmly shook mine. His eyes and face were more eloquent than his words in asking for forgiveness. If I still harbored any doubts about the purpose of his rescue undertakings, his candid words issuing straight from the heart dispelled them completely.

It was such extraordinary, thoroughly humane persons that our sages had in mind when they wrote: "The righteous of the nations of the world have a portion in the world to come."

Meanwhile September was drawing to a close. The bloody year 1942–43 was about to end.

On Saturday night, September 1943, Jews in the free world were probably getting ready to recite Selikhot [penitential prayers recited on the Jewish New Year].

The first day of the New Year fell on Tuesday, September 30, and Yom Kippur was due on October 9. Since I kept accurate account of holy days and festivals, I was able to commune in my thoughts with the community of Israel. No holy place, no public prayer, no prayer book, and no Jews. I was alone, set apart and cast out. I spent the Days of Awe in the very heart of the Uniate Catholic church. "From the depths I call on thee, O Lord." With these words I poured out my heart before the Eternal God.

On a cold and rainy day in late October 1943, Hrtzai again informed me that I would have to leave the palace and return to the monastery at Piotr Skarga Street. There was fear in the air, the front lines kept moving westward and there were too many Germans going in and out of the metropolitan's office. Under these circumstances I would be safer in the Studite monastery. So I must wander again. I asked only one question: When was I due to be transferred?

Brother Teodosy, the same dear friend Teodosy, played the part of the smuggler. Again he was risking his life to smuggle me into the monastery.

The night was dark and rainy. Teodosy removed the sliding boards of the partition of my attic hideout. I bent and went inside.

Again I was shut in my hideout. The days and nights were cold and gloomy. The rain drummed on the sheet iron roof and its drops fell like tears of sorrow on my soul, swaddling it in layers of dejection. Cold moisture penetrated my bones. I trembled with cold, my temperature rose, I coughed. Before I knew it I was down with a cold. Summoning a doctor would have entailed mortal risk.

Teodosy moved me to a cell adjacent to the staircase on the third floor. The cell was heated with an iron stove. I lay on a clean, warm bed. It had been a long time since I saw a bed. I was brought an aspirin and hot tea. As usual, Teodosy attended to my needs.

Several days later I recovered.

In the Library of the Monastery

In early November 1943, the abbot of the Studite monastery, Father Nikanor, paid me a visit. He greeted me warmly and conveyed regards from my wife and daughter. He informed me that within a few days I would be transferred to the large library room called the "Studyon." I would have a bunk in a corner of the library and would work with the monk Titus Prostyuk on cataloging the library collections. The Studyon library is adjacent to the monastery and forms an integral part of it. It occupies two floors and contains thousands of volumes. This large theological library specializes in Byzantine studies; Byzantine Christianity gave birth to the Uniate Catholic church. Ukrainian literature and history, as well as philosophy, are also amply represented. Judaic studies take up a corner of their own in the library: Jewish history, Bible studies, Hebrew literature, Talmud and halakic rulings, Midrashim, prayer books, and so on. One can also find books by Jewish writers such as Sholem-Aleykhem, Mendele, Peretz, and others, in the original. The library is connected to the monastery building by a long passage ending with a locked door, which settled the question of safety.

As usual, it was the friendly brother Teodosy who guided me to the library. He also took care of my safety. I was accommodated in a concealed corner of the library, which contained a bed, a table, a chair, and an electric stove. But its most important feature was a bunker concealed behind the thick volumes of the Byzantine library. When in danger, all I had to do was remove several thick volumes from the shelf and crawl into a narrow but comfortable and well-concealed bunker. The monks also provided me with an alarm system in the form of an electric bell. Upon hearing five rings I was to enter the bunker immediately.

Two sleeping boards were placed in my corner. The second, as it turned out, was designated for a boy, Nathan Lewin, the youngest son of Rabbi Ezekiel Lewin. The boy had been moved from one place to another until the metropolitan decided to entrust him to my custody. His assumed name was Bogdan Levitsky.

Several days later Teodosy brought the boy to me, an eleven-year-old with blue, clear, but frightened, eyes; sweet, kind, good-hearted, patient, smart, and alert to everything going on around him. He was a great comfort to me in those dark days.

The second person with whom I was destined to spend the winter in the library was the monk Titus Prostyuk. He was a middle-aged man, very tall, with a black beard and piercing eyes. He wore the simple black robe of the monks and the tall, pointed hood of the Studite order. He was a serious, thorough, and friendly man, always ready to come to the aid of others. He was very sensitive to human suffering, especially to the sufferings of the Jews. He was also a priest, a graduate of a theological seminary, with a university education, a scholar devoted to reading; he evinced particular interest in biblical studies.

Our first meeting was very friendly. He said: "In my work in the library, most of all I desire to be at your service, to help you in your difficult situation, and to make your forcible confinement as bearable as possible. Our assignment is to prepare the library catalog. I am sure this work will help you to regain your composure and soothe your nerves."

Titus spoke to me in Ukrainian. By that time I spoke Ukrainian well and read it fluently.

This is how I opened a new chapter in my confinement, in the Studyon library in the company of Titus.

In the course of time I began teaching him Hebrew. He was a diligent pupil and within a relatively short time was able to read a simple biblical passage and translate it.

Work in the library among books had a calming effect on me; it soothed my frayed nerves and injected a modicum of vitality and hope. I read a great deal. Every evening I spent several hours in the corner with the Judaica books, studying a chapter of Talmud with *tosaphoth*. I also read books on the history of the Jewish people, or to be more exact, I studied the history of Jewish martyrology, a subject close to my heart at that time.

Titus and I also began translating the Book of Psalms into modern Ukrainian. We spent many hours on the translation. He planned to publish the Ukrainian translation in which I helped him a great deal.

In mid-November 1943 a new tenant came to live in the monastery: Kurt Lewin, the eldest son of Rabbi Ezekiel Lewin. In the middle of summer 1942 he had come to the metropolitan, asking for shelter for himself and his brother. This took place after my and Rabbi Chameides's visit to the metropolitan. To recall, our visit at that time, during which we reported to the metropolitan on the situation of the Jewish population, was the direct cause of a large rescue operation launched by the metropolitan. Kurt and his younger brother were received with open arms by the priest Kotiv who from then on attended to their every need. Kurt, who had gone through many ordeals before he reached Lvov, lived under the assumed name of Roman Mitka as stated in his

Aryan papers. Father Rafail, the abbot of one of the monasteries where he had sought shelter, ordered him to be removed for a simple reason: he did not want to hide Jews. The fate that was befalling the Jews, he said, indicated that God wanted the Jewish people to be exterminated and God supported the extermination. Anyone helping Jews acted against the will of God. It is to be noted that Rafail was among the more intelligent priests, educated, well read, a talented painter, and endowed with artistic gifts. Thus it seems that the metropolitan and his circle did not succeed in exerting their influence and authority over all the priests.

Ultimately Kurt succeeded in finding refuge in the Carpathian mountains at the small, remote Lozki monastery. There were seven anchorite monks, Abbot Nikanor and six brothers in the monastery. At the end of November Kurt arrived in Lvov. Now the three of us—Titus, Kurt, and I—worked in the library.

In early December we had our first experience of alarm. At 8:00 P.M. the electric bell rang five times—an alert. A search must be under way. Nathan and I immediately went inside our bunker behind the bookshelves. As a holder of proper papers, Kurt, who wore monastic robes, had nothing to fear. One minute later we heard the German visitors entering the library in the company of Abbot Nikanor.

Inspection of the library lasted half an hour. The Germans opened all the closets and inspected papers and catalogs. They passed near our hideout but nothing aroused their suspicion. The concealment was perfect.

During the winter of 1943–44 we went through six searches. Six times we heard the bell ringing. Six times we experienced the dreaded close calls of hiding Jews. The Germans, however, never suspected anything.

At the end of December 1943, I was treated to a surprise. The head of all the Studite convents, Abbess Iosefa, brought my little daughter to the library. Her assumed name was Romcia. I am hard pressed for words to describe our meeting. I clasped her to my heart and for a long time was unable to utter a word. The child too was visibly moved. She appraised me silently with the seriousness of a four-year-old. Her eyes had the look of a grown-up person. All ghetto children had the same expression in their eyes; that which they could not comprehend with their minds, they grasped intuitively with their senses. After a long silence, when I could sense the voice of her heart and she began nestling against me, I could not restrain myself any longer and asked the dangerous question which could have cost me my life: "Do you know who I am, Romcia?" She replied softly, warily, in Ukrainian: "You are my father." I could barely hear her voice. I held her tightly against my breast and we both kept silent. Our hearts communed in their wordless language.

We were alone in the library at that time. When the abbess took the girl away, I remained numb and dejected. The wound was opened once again. My nerves, soothed somewhat by the daily library routine, became overwrought once again. I felt derailed. It took me a full week to regain my previous composure.

The winter with its sorrow and anguish passed. I worked in the library and slept with Nathan in our hideout, near the bunker concealed by books. All day I worked with Titus and Kurt in arranging books and composing a catalog of the huge Byzantine library. At nighttime I read a great deal, drawing comfort from the books in the Judaica corner. I remember one evening in the middle of February 1944 which transported me away from my world, the monastery, the hideout, in short, from all my surroundings. Browsing through the Judaica books, I came across a tale in Gemarah Taanith (22), saying that in times of emergency and danger, Jews would take off their characteristic garments and dress in Gentile clothes so as not to be recognized. I found a similar story in Midrash Rabba. Our Aryan papers, Gentile dress, this whole masquerade, was designed to save our lives. Although the present disaster was unprecedented in our history, the steps Jews had to take to save their lives did not change.

From time to time Abbot Nikanor paid me a visit. He was a very congenial man, loving and considerate, always dispensing words of hope. The front lines are getting nearer and nearer, he said. The German army is close to collapse. And in fact, cannons could be heard distinctly near Tarnopol. Even from here gleams can be seen. We must hold out, place our trust in God, and hope for redemption.

I received news from the outside world from Kurt who enjoyed freedom of movement with his monastic robes and proper papers. The kind Brother Teodosy also visited me often, bringing news of special interest to me, namely reports concerning Jews. Most of them were deeply distressing. A bunker with hiding Jews was discovered and its occupants shot. In several places Christian families were shot together with the Jews they had been sheltering. He also informed me that the Janowski camp continued to operate under a new commandant, Warzog. Atrocities in the camp had not abated; on the contrary, they had reached new heights. Jews from all over eastern Galicia were being brought there to be murdered. Instead of dying out, the hellfire kept raging.

By the end of April, signs of German retreat and the imminent collapse of the German army multiplied. The Soviets began bombarding Lvov. One morning Titus informed me that my wife was due to visit me on Sunday. Apparently, at Jura Mountain they decided that the time had come for our meeting. Until then I received only spare reports about her; fear of informers prevented relaying more detailed information. On Sunday morning, about 10:00 A.M., my wife came to the monastery accompanied by Abbess Iosefa. Presently she told me her story.

She left the ghetto after Yom Kippur 1942. She was not in good health; alone she had had to face a hostile and suspicious world. She found her first refuge at the convent in the Liczakow district, located at Obucz alley, at the residence of the head of all the Studite convents, Abbess Iosefa (Helena Witter). Iosefa is an intelligent woman, of refined sensibility, vigorous but also nervous. About forty years old, she rules the convents under her jurisdiction, in which she had introduced order and discipline, with a firm hand and an intimate knowledge of the human mind. The Studite order had established an extensive network of monasteries and convents, charity institutions, and children's homes.

In this area the Studites competed with the older and more established Basilian order. The Studites enjoyed the full support of the metropolitan, even though in the past he himself had been a Basilian monk. The wise rule of Abbess Iosefa could be clearly felt in the institutions under her authority. Having left the ghetto, my wife was sent by the abbess to the convent in Brzuchowice where she learned Ukrainian and acquainted herself with the surroundings, the people, the customs, and the dangers of her new situation. She was furnished with original and reliable Aryan papers. By and by she accustomed herself to the ways of the non-Jewish world, to the street, so that she even summoned the courage to go outside without an escort.

As I have mentioned earlier, acting on the instructions of the metropolitan, the priest Kotiv gathered Jewish children from towns and villages, and with the help of Abbess Iosefa delivered them to the care of convents and various charitable institutions of the Studite order. The abbess received the children personally, ensured their safety, and accommodated them in various convents.

This whole venture exposed those involved to enormous risks, but Iosefa carried on with great determination, saying that it was a Christian duty.

At a children's home near the convent in Brzuchowice, many Jewish children were being educated. My wife used to visit Brzuchowice, asking for the names of the children and committing them to memory. She had a very difficult time then. The Lvov ghetto was ruled by the blood-thirsty Grzymek and the Janowski camp by Willhaus. She knew that her husband was in the camp and her sister in the Jewish barracks at the Lvov railway station. These barracks formed a separate camp for Jewish forced labor workers who lived there in dreadful conditions. Displaying great courage, my wife used to leave Brzuchowice and walk near the camp, hoping to pass a note to me. This she succeeded in accomplishing. But the most trying time for her was in mid-January 1943, during the January *Aktion*.

In January 1943, Jewish Lvov, the reduced and shriveled ghetto, was the scene of one of the most bloody *Aktionen* ever unleashed against the Jews of Lvov. Before loading their victims onto the trains bound for Belzec, the Germans were stripping them practically naked. In early January, on the Ukrainian Christmas day (Byzantine churches celebrate Christmas after the Christmas of Catholics) at night, my wife set out in the company of several nuns from the church to the residence of the Brzuchowice vicar Leszczynski. The place was near the railway line from Lvov to Belzec. It was a freezing winter night and a snow storm was raging. Just before 10:00 P.M., as the nuns were about to set out on the way back to the convent, they heard shouts, cries, and knocks on the windows: "Please open up, have pity on us, let us in!"

Outside there was a group of Jews, either completely or partially naked, who had jumped off the train to Belzec. They pleaded to be allowed inside.

Father Leszczynski was seized by panic and went pale. He opened the door himself but did not let anyone in. Instead he brought them clothes, shoes, and food. He was too scared to let them into his house. Who can describe what went on in the mind of a Jewish woman witnessing this scene?

Next morning, when the Christian residents of Brzuchowice went to church to celebrate Christmas, they could see numerous blood stains along the railway tracks, as well as frozen, snow-covered bodies strewn on both sides of the tracks. Although she was fainting with pain, on the verge of going insane, the Jewish woman could not as much as change her expression at the sight of her brethren lying there, for fear she herself might share their fate.

In March 1943 my wife left Brzuchowice. A prolonged stay in one place exposed her to risk. After her return to Lvov she stayed for a short while in the convent at Obucz Street. Subsequently she began working in the municipal infant care center at Ostrowski Street. Professor Grer, a well-known pediatrician in Lvov, had worked in this institution before the war. By that time the Grer Institute was converted into an infant care center. My wife worked there as a nursemaid. The term "work," however, does not convey her situation. Great efforts, precautions, and ploys were required on her part in order for her to remain inconspicuous, doing minor work so as to lessen the risk of someone taking an interest in her. She was always afraid, always on guard, lest she disclose her true identity by an inadvertent expression or a sigh. It was difficult then to be a Jewish woman on Aryan papers. My wife maintained close contact with Abbess Iosefa; she visited her often and received news from her about her daughter and husband. She knew I was alive and under good protection, but she did not know where I was.

On one of her visits to the abbess in the convent at Obucz Street in the winter of 1944, she saw two girls there, ten and five years old. The small one had a deep bullet wound above the knee. Both girls were dirty and infested with lice. The abbess treated them with her own hands. She cleaned the wound of pus, washed their hair, disinfected them with kerosene, and gave them a bath in her own washroom. The two little Jewish girls had jumped off the train to Belzec. The smaller one was shot by an S.S. man guarding the train. The older girl was not injured; she dragged her smaller companion to the nearest village where luckily they fell into the hands of good people who brought them to the monastery in Lvov. When my wife asked the abbess to let her wash the girls, she replied: "I am doing my duty and I am doing it to fulfill a commandment. I want to fulfill this commandment all by myself, without any help." The girls survived and subsequently were sent to a convent in eastern Galicia. The older girl was given the name Wladka and the younger—Leicha.

This incident was like a ray of light on a dark, overcast, and gloomy day. But such rays only rarely burst through the clouds. The air was permeated with hostility, hatred, and contempt: "Unbearable as it is, the German occupation has at least one good thing going for it. At long last we shall be rid of the Jews and for this Hitler deserves a statue. . . ."

Slowly, in tense expectation, the summer months of May and June 1944 passed. Lvov suffered heavy bombardment nearly every day. Everyone including the Germans saw the approaching end. Hitler's defeat was inevitable. But Jew-hatred did not abate even for a moment.

In early May Teodosy told me about a Jewish bunker which was uncovered in the cemetery, in the depths of a family vault. Twenty-eight Jews were removed from there and shot. Who informed on them? Who would conceivably inform on hiding Jews in the last days of Hitler's rule? How deep is the hatred. As it is written: "Halakah determined: Esau hates Jacob."

June–July 1944. The front line reached the city. Bombardments intensify with each passing day. I am forbidden to seek shelter in the cellar; too many tenants from all the houses in the neighborhood go down there during bombardments. Filled with gratitude I sit upstairs in the library. I tremble with fear, but my heart is filled with hope.

On July 27, 1944, Lvov was liberated. The Red Army took over the city. At long last I am free again like any other man.

⅍ APPENDIX I

Two Accounts of Rabbi Lewin's Death

There are two accounts of Rabbi Lewin's death. The first was given by an eyewitness, Elyahu Jonas, in his book entitled "On the edge of the pit" (published in Hebrew [Jerusalem, 1957]):

A group of Jews, their faces to the wall, stood on the other side of the yard. "Who are they?" I asked my neighbors. I was told that these were prominent figures of the Jewish Lvov community: public servants, intellectuals, respected leaders, etc. The rioting crowds had removed them from their homes and brought them here. The Germans were holding them here as a separate group. They had been standing like that, facing the wall, for the whole day. Only in the evening were they suddenly transferred here.

Rabbi Lewin, the rabbi of the Lvov community, brother of the well-known Rabbi Lewin of Rzeszow, was in this group. I remember him very well. He was a man of medium height and a small beard adorned his noble face. When he was placed among us, he lost his composure the moment he saw our swollen faces and our soiled, blood-stained clothes. He stood next to me. I wore summer clothes and my sleeves were rolled. The rabbi clutched my hand as if asking for help and to draw some strength. Suddenly some Germans approached him and one of them barked an order: "Let the barber come!" Before we could grasp the meaning of his words, two soldiers held him by the arms and the third started plucking out his beard, the way one plucks out feathers from a slaughtered hen. He held himself in check for a few seconds and then began screaming. As they tortured him, he kept holding my hand with an enormous strength; it was impossible to break his hold on me. I did not try to. I felt I was somehow helping him. He kept on screaming. Then his knees went weak, he fell on the ground, stopped screaming, and let go of my hand.

At that moment I blended in with the crowd and started pushing my way through the throng. Some inner force kept driving me on and on. I kept walking, the rabbi's voice haunting me as if in a dream, until I found myself in an empty, smoke-filled hallway. I kept on walking until I reached

153

a barred window. I pulled one bar and it gave way. Pieces of burnt plaster fell on my head and face. I waited for a few moments and then jumped out of the window without giving much thought to what could happen to me.

The second account was given by Rabbi Lewin's son Itzhak in his book, "I came to Israel from Spezia [a harbor in Italy]" (published in Hebrew, by Am Oved Publishers, Tel-Aviv, 1947).

At the time of riots in the city, the "Brygidki" was but a smouldering ruin. Only the prison cellars, where the Soviets had hidden thousands of corpses and then sealed the openings, remained intact. When the cellars were opened, an unbearable stench rose up from them. In the heat of the sun it became suffocating. Oh, how unbearable is the smell of decomposing human flesh! The henchmen, who could not stand it, put on gas masks. They split us up into two groups. One group was put to work in breaking through the sealed openings. The second group pulled up the corpses by rope from the cellars and laid them on the lawn of the yard. The bodies were covered with pus and often a hand or a leg fell away from the body. Their faces were twisted in a terrible fashion, the convulsions of death still visible on them. The skin on some of the corpses had disappeared. The work was dreadful and the malice of the German taskmasters made it even worse. Gestapo men, plain soldiers, and Ukrainians hit us right and left with rifle butts, iron bars, and knouts. Those who fell under the blows were stamped upon their faces, chests, or stomachs until they gave their last breath. I remember one of these Ukrainians, who was dressed in the traditional embroidered shirt and elegant jacket. He hit us with an iron stick. Later his beating became methodical and he hit us even on the head. Each blow tore pieces of flesh from our bodies. He gouged out some people's eyes, and he tore off others' ears. When his stick broke, without thinking much, he grabbed a burning coal and hit my neighbor on the head with it. The skull was crushed open and his brain splattered all over, wetting my face and my clothes. The poor victim died instantly. Breathing heavily, the Ukrainian murderer leaned against the wall to rest a bit. His rapacious face, his red eyes, swollen veins and glands presented an odious and repulsive sight.

In the meantime, the Ukrainian militia herded in fresh victims. Among them were my friend from school, Henryk Zysman, his father, and his brother. Henryk's brother was told to stand against the wall and his head was riddled with bullets. Thereupon the father and son were ordered to remove the body and place it on the heap of bodies of murdered Jews in the corner. Upon their return the father and son were separated and Henryk was shot to death. He only managed to shout to his father "Farewell!" Under the impact of the death of his two sons the father broke down and went insane. In despair he began howling. Ultimately he left the Brygidki alive, only to die slowly over the course of a year, in the ghetto.

At ten o'clock I suddenly saw my father. He was pushed by two Germans who kept hitting him with rifle butts. Pale as a ghost, wearing priestly robes, he walked to his death. How can I describe my bitterness and despair, the despair of a small child helplessly beholding the murder of his father. In utter despair and helplessness, I tore my clothes and my hair. Then something in me snapped and I was struck numb. I just kept staring. As my father passed between groups of Jews he recited the confessional prayer and said in a loud voice: "Shema Israel" (Hear O Israel!). At that time the Germans opened fire into this corner. All those who worked in removing the corpses from the cellars heard his prayer, the prayer of martyrs and innocents being murdered by villains. They joined him and all at once the din and clatter of shots was drowned in the powerful sound of Shema Israel. The threats and blows failed to stop our prayer which infused us with a superhuman strength.

An Account of the Rabbis' Meeting
with Dr. Landesberg

In a book by Polish writer Tadeusz Zaderecki, *Gdy swastyka Lwowem wladala* (When swastika ruled over Lvov), there is a passage purporting to describe the meeting of rabbis with Dr. Landesberg. According to Zaderecki the rabbis' reply was: "If so, let the Gestapo take the people, but you and the Judenrat officials must not hand them over." "I will not sacrifice myself for somebody else," said Landesberg. "This is exactly what you must do!" was the rabbis' reply.

Zaderecki heard the story of the delegation of rabbis to Landesberg from me in August 1944, shortly after the liberation of Lvov. I recounted to him these events and read him my notes in Yiddish. The meeting is described in this book very briefly and I find it necessary to expand it in view of some errors which crept into Zaderecki's account.

For two full days the rabbis deliberated on the halakic precedents in similar cases. The following sources were mentioned: Babylonian Talmud, Treatise Terumoth, chapter 8, Mishna 12; Jerusalem Talmud, Terumoth, ruling 4; Maimonides, Halakhot Yesod Hatorah, chapter 5, ruling 5; Midrash Bereshit Rabba, chapter 94:9 (end of the portion); Shulkhan Arukh–Yoreh Deah, 157:1, and others. The rabbis' confusion was compounded by rumors saying that a certain number of Jews had to be handed over to the Germans so as to save the others in the ghetto. Should the Judenrat acquiesce in their demand, it would be able to carry out this business as mercifully as possible, whereas the Germans would do the same thing with their customary cruelty and murder-lust.

Ultimately, it was decided to hold an official meeting and discuss this issue with all due seriousness. The brief session was chaired by the eldest, Rabbi Israel Leib Wolfsberg, and was attended by all the rabbis. The atmosphere was gloomy and depressing. We all felt the weight of the responsiblity that was resting on our shoulders. The rabbis rejected the principle of saving many by sacrificing a few. They took into consideration the opinion of Tamudic sages (Treatise Sanhedrin, 74a and Pesachim, 25b): "Why should you regard your blood as more red than the blood of others and your life as more worthy than the life of others? Perhaps the opposite is true? One soul is not better than the other."

Rabbi Alter launched a strongly worded attack on the Judenrat for its failure to ask our opinion on this grave matter. It was decided unanimously to dispatch a delegation to Landesberg. The account of the meeting with Landesberg as given in my diary is a truthful one. Rabbi Wolfsberg was the only speaker. The rabbis did not quote the ruling which appears in Shulkhan Arukh–Yoreh Deah, Hilkhot Akum, paragraph 157. Instead they conveyed to him the precis of the ruling by Maimonides (Halakhot Yesod Hatorah, chapter 5, ruling 5) without mentioning the name of the author. They underscored the immense responsibility Landesberg would assume by complying with the German orders. Landesberg replied as he did. No arguments were exchanged and certainly he did not say, as Zaderecki claims: "I will not sacrifice myself for somebody else." He said nothing of the sort. By putting these words in his mouth, we wrong the man who battled enough with his conscience and ultimately paid with his life. At the time of our meeting he was a broken and exhausted man who took the decision after terrible inner struggle and who did not have enough strength to rise to the level of his predecessor, Dr. Yosef Parnas.

As for the halakic ruling: as a matter of fact there is no halakic work that systematically discusses this grave subject. At no period in its history did the people of Israel face a similar situation. The main sources for halakic ruling on the matter in question consist of books of questions and answers written in the aftermath of disasters visited upon the Jewish people, beginning with the decrees of Hadrian (117–138 CE), the persecutions of the Crusades (1096–1215), decrees of apostasy in Christian Spain in the fourteenth century, and the violence unleashed by Khmelnytskyi in the Ukraine (1648–49). No valid comparison can be made, however, between these calamities and the total disaster of the Holocaust. The former had to do with forcible conversion, whereas during the Holocaust the Jewish people were meant to be totally annihilated.

Thou Shalt Not Murder

From the 1941 Pastoral Letter of
Metropolitan Andrei Sheptytskyi

The Christian church tirelessly reminds all the faithful of their duties as Christians, the foremost of which is the observance of God's commandments. But there are times when it is of utmost importance for society that we must insist on these duties more solemnly and with special emphasis. *We strongly feel that we live in such times—times when people are in danger of forgetting the laws of God,* times when sins multiply, when sins are being committed arrogantly and ostentatiously, without encountering any resistance from Christians. This disregard for the sacrosanct commandments of God, this disrespect of the Divine, expressing itself above all in disobeying His sublime will, represents a great tragedy and poses a great danger to everyone. For violation of God's commandments may and will bring about God's punishment— *the greatest of troubles and the greatest of misfortunes for humanity.*

It is with dread that we observe growing signs of the forsaking of God's commandments among the faithful entrusted by Him into our care. Moved by deep solicitude and anxiety over the eternal and terrestrial happiness of the people so dear to us, we undertake an unceasing search after ways and means to awaken the people's memory of their duties toward God. With this in mind we have convened an archiepiscopal synod in which we presented for discussion and decision a number of edicts concerning God's commandments. The Synod of 1941 discussed the first three commandments and matters relating to the Fourth Commandment. The archiepiscopal Synod of 1942 assigned six formal sessions to the continuation of work begun in 1941 and was devoted to a number of rules concerning the Fourth Commandment. The synod conducted its proceedings at a slower pace than we hoped to achieve. In our effort to bring the full weight of the synod's decisions to bear on the deliberations concerning the Fifth Commandment, from the beginning of this year we have issued pastoral letters aimed at drawing the attention of esteemed clergymen and of our dear people to the great importance of observing the commandment of loving one's neighbor, as well as the immeasurable danger of violating the commandment "Thou shalt not murder."

Our edicts on this matter were read at the preliminary sessions of the archiepiscopal synod of November 26, 1942, and December 3, 1942. At these two sessions we discussed the rules through which the observation of this commandment can and must be emphasized. It was further decided that part of the rules pertaining to our edicts would be brought up for discussion at the solemn meeting of the synod due to be convened on December 12, 1942. These rules, however, are far from comprehensive for a subject as important as this. We have therefore decided to issue a solemn pastoral letter to high-ranking clergymen and to the Christians in our dioceses, *in order to fulfill our duty to the Almighty as shepherds of souls and preachers of the Gospel, to warn our faithful, with heaven and earth as our witnesses, against the evil deeds which have recently spread among us so frightfully, and call for penitence on the part of persons who committed the sin of murder.*

In what follows we shall endeavor to describe briefly the importance, sanctity, and greatness of God's commandment: Thou shalt love thy neighbor as thyself. We seek to contrast this heavenly image—the essence of loving the Creator and morality—with the dreadful crime of murder. In its essence, this crime is directly and severely opposed to the most sacrosanct human obligations, whose fulfillment can assure happiness in this world and eternal life.

Beloved brethren: First, it is our duty to remind you that loving one's neighbor is the core of Jesus' teaching as expressed in his saying: "Beloved, let us love one another: for love is of God; and every one that loveth is born of God, and knoweth God. He that loveth not knoweth not God; for God is love" (First Epistle of John, 4:7–8).

By transgressing the Fifth Commandment "Thou shalt not murder" one commits a most horrid and heinous crime, forsakes and uproots from himself the most holy of all, the Christian love of one's neighbor which embraces every living thing. A murderer casts himself out of God's congregation, namely the human family as God conceived it. Through this grave sin toward human society the murderer removes himself from it and subjects himself to the severest punishment by God in the world to come, as well as bringing upon his head a terrible curse in this world.

Just as in his books of revelation, almost at the beginning, God presented Cain's sin and the curse. He cursed him as a memorial of admonition and reproach and as a terrifying example, so He enshrined his will of law, order, and system in the commandment "Thou shalt not murder." This means that every social arrangement, according to the recognition and respect of Divine authority, is founded on the indisputable sanctity of human life. The Master of the world protects this sanctity and says to anyone trying to subvert it: "What hast thou done? The voice of thy brother's blood crieth unto Me from the ground. And now art thou cursed from the earth, which hath opened her mouth to receive thy brother's blood from thy hand; when thou tillest the ground, it shall not henceforth yield unto thee her strength; a fugitive and vagabond shalt thou be on the earth." This divine verdict strikes like lightning at anyone who slights God's commandment by shedding innocent blood and thereby casts himself out of human society, because he has not honored the supreme value of this society, namely, human life.

The brand of the curse burned into the body of a murderer is but an outward mark of the grave sin committed by such an unfortunate soul. In the dark chambers of the murderer's soul things come to pass which were so powerfully described in the Book of Psalms: "My wounds stink and are corrupt because of my foolishness. I am troubled; I am bowed down greatly; I go mourning all the day long. For my loins are filled with a loathsome disease: and there is no soundness in my flesh. I am feeble and sore broken: I have roared by reason of the disquietness of my heart" (38:6–9). "Set thou a wicked man over him: and let Satan stand at his right Hand. When he shall be judged, let him be condemned: and let his prayer become sin. Let his days be few; and let another take his office. Let his children be fatherless, and his wife a widow. Let his children be continually vagabonds, and beg: let them seek their bread also out of their desolate places. Let the executioner catch all that he hath; and let the strangers spoil his labor. Let there be none to extend mercy unto him: neither let there be any to favor his fatherless children" (109:6–12).

The Book of Psalms uses these terrible terms to describe the accursed condition awaiting a murderer. This fate awaits a murderer in this world, whereas Satan and his assistants wait for him in the hereafter (Matthew 25:41).

Those who do not regard politically motivated murder as a crime commit an astonishing error; as if politics exempts a man from his duties toward God's commandments, as if it is capable of justifying natural crime. But this is not so. A Christian must observe God's commandments not only in his private life, but, above all, in public and political life. A man shedding the blood of his political rival or foe is every inch a murderer, just as is a man killing another out of greed, and he deserves the same punishment from heaven and the same anathema of the Church.

Not only a Christian but everyone among us is bound by the duty to love one's neighbor by virtue of his human nature. Our Lord Jesus Christ, the judge of justice, sits in judgment not only over the Christians, but over all men according to their deeds, above all, according to deeds of kindness and love for one's neighbor, as it is described in the vision of the End of Days.

A murderer is revealed as lacking mercy not only toward the poor, the suffering, and the captive; he also does unto his fellow man the worst thing he can do, since he deprives him of his life—perhaps at the moment his victim is not prepared to face death and has no hope to gain eternal life.

The act of murder inflicts irreparable damage on the children, wife, and elderly parents of the victim. Deprived of their breadwinner, they have been left to starve and suffer. A murderer takes the life not only of his victim, but also robs his own soul of the prospect of eternal life and God's grace, thereby leading it to an abyss from which there is no escape. The curse of the shedding of innocent blood stirs to life the demons of greed in his soul, who from now on goad him to seek gratification of his desires in the suffering and torment of his fellow man.

The sight of spilt blood arouses in him the lust associated with cruelty, which can be satisfied only through the agonies of the victim and his death. Bloodthirstiness can become transformed into lust which will derive pleasure from tormenting the victim and his death. A murderer who attains this level of bloodthirstiness and who takes sadistic pleasure from torments, torture, and death, unquestionably becomes a danger to his fellow man. For him crime becomes a necessity. Without crime he suffers and undergoes unceasing torments, just as a man deprived of food and drink suffers hunger and thirst. Those forced to live in close proximity to such a person must be constantly on guard. Children might disappear and crimes might be committed and often it proves impossible to uncover the perpetrators. Responsible public bodies will have to go to the greatest lengths to denounce such a depraved person who has forshaken all humanity, and bring him to justice.

In a letter of March 27, 1942, the Ordinariat of the metropolitan prescribed for murderers the punishment reserved to the Ordinariat: excommunication. Although this punishment does not require Christians to completely boycott the excommunicated person, nonetheless shepherds of souls are required to explain faithfully to their flocks the meaning of this punishment and its consequences so that all the faithful together with their spiritual guide will be able to participate in the repentance and mending of ways on the part of the unfortunate person who has brought such punishment upon his head. Through remonstrating with him constantly, through severing all prescribed social connections with him, and through total severing of all family ties, they must explain to the murderer that they regard him as a danger to the entire congregation, a plague that it must avoid lest it strike it. If all members of the congregation will refrain from greeting the criminal, from letting him into their homes, from speaking to him; if all members of his family will display reservations about kinship relations with him; if people will refrain from sitting next to him in the church; if everyone will avoid meeting him in the street; if no one will sell to him or buy from him—perhaps then he would mend his ways and begin a life of repentance and improvement. Confessors must go to the greatest lengths to enable the repentant criminals to reap the blessed harvest of their repentance. Should the priest come to the conclusion that he can lawfully lift from the sinner the yoke of excommunication, he might well remember that the required penance for the act of murder must correspond to the monstrosity of such a crime. Should the crime recur and should the mind of the criminal reveal sadistic inclinations, and the crime has become public knowledge, the priest must impose not only a heavy penance, but also a penance that will fit the sense of justice of the people.